MW00443280

THE ART OF
Quilling Paper
JEWELRY

**TECHNIQUES & PROJECTS FOR
METALLIC EARRINGS & PENDANTS**

—

ANN MARTIN

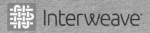

The Art of Quilling Paper Jewelry
Copyright © 2017 by Ann Martin.
Manufactured in China. All rights
reserved. No part of this book may
be reproduced in any form or by
any electronic or mechanical means
including information storage and
retrieval systems without permission in
writing from the publisher, except by a
reviewer who may quote brief passages
in a review. Published by Interweave
Books, an imprint of F+W Media, Inc.,
10151 Carver Road, Suite 200, Blue
Ash, Ohio 45242. (800) 289-0963.
First Edition.

fw
a content + ecommerce company

www.fwcommunity.com

21 20 19 18 17 5 4 3 2 1

Distributed in Canada
by Fraser Direct
100 Armstrong Avenue
Georgetown, ON, Canada
L7G 5S4
Tel: (905) 877-4411

Distributed in the U.K. and Europe
by F&W MEDIA INTERNATIONAL
Pynes Hill Court, Pynes Hill,
Rydon Lane Exeter, EX2 5AZ,
United Kingdom
Tel: (+44) 1392 797680
E-mail: enquiries@fwmedia.com

SRN: 17JM02

ISBN-13: 978-1-63250-577-4

Editorial Director: Kerry Bogert

Editors: Jodi Butler and Erica Smith

Technical Editor: Bonnie Brooks

Art Director: Ashlee Wadeson

Cover & Interior Designer:
Pamela Norman

Illustrator: Bonnie Brooks

Photographer: George Boe

Contents

Introduction

Welcome to the world of quilled jewelry, one of my very favorite uses of the time-honored art of paper filigree, more commonly known as quilling. This paper-rolling technique has been in existence for hundreds of years and has changed remarkably little in all of that time. Narrow strips of paper are still rolled around a slim tool to create elegant coils and scrolls that can be combined in nearly limitless ways. While nuns and monks prepared gilded paper to decorate religious relics during the Renaissance instead of more costly metal filigree, quillers today can take advantage of beautiful and readily available machine-cut strips onto which gold, silver, or copper paint has been applied along one edge.

Stunning, yet inexpensive metallic-edge paper is used to create all of the contemporary jewelry projects in this book. Of course, plain quilling paper can be used as well, but trust me, specialty strips with their brilliant shine turn each piece into a conversation starter. Use it to make a surprisingly sturdy pendant or pair of earrings tonight and wear your finished jewelry tomorrow. I predict you'll gather admiring glances and compliments!

While quilling may seem intimidating at first, I'll let you in on a little secret. Each of the twenty projects in this book is made with a mix of only a handful of different coils and scrolls, which are rolled on a tool exactly the same way. And in case you are doubtful, as I was the first time I was introduced to quilling, paper can most definitely be made to stand on edge. Via step-by-step tutorials, you will learn how best to handle short lengths of paper and pinch them into familiar shapes, such as teardrops and marquises. Whether you are an accomplished jewelry artist or a novice crafter, you have the ability to create gift-worthy jewelry.

Even though there is much repetition technique-wise in the included projects, the magic of quilling is revealed in the incredible variety of modern designs. I should also mention that once the basics are learned, the rolling and shaping process becomes a delightfully relaxing zone. Add to that the satisfaction that comes from using your hands to create beautiful, long-lasting jewelry that will be cherished for years.

Quilling requires very few supplies, so you'll be able to create these pieces at a relatively small cost. If you simply can't wait to get started or are hesitant to seek out supplies before giving paper rolling a try, run a piece of printer paper through a shredder to make practice strips and grab a bottle of craft glue. Any thin, stiff wire will suffice as a tool.

As you may have already guessed, one more requirement is a fair amount of patience. Keep in mind that with several practice sessions, your coils will become smoothly rolled and evenly sized. Revel in the fact that in time you will be able to do something that many have never even heard of, but that's about to change the moment you wear a newly minted quilled pendant or pair of earrings and introduce your extraordinary art to everyone you meet!

Ann

CHAPTER ONE

Materials & Tools

Simple (and simply beautiful) strips of quilling paper, a short list of tools (many of which you probably have on hand), and a bit of patience are all you will need to get started making your own showstopping jewelry.

Materials

QUILLING PAPER

Quilling paper is readily available as precut strips, and some colors can be purchased in sheet form. In general, quilling paper is a bit thicker and softer to the touch than regular printer paper. The weight of the strips featured in this book, for example, is generally 100 or 120 gsm (grams per square meter). In comparison, printer paper weighs 80 to 90 gsm, while cardstock is 170 gsm and higher.

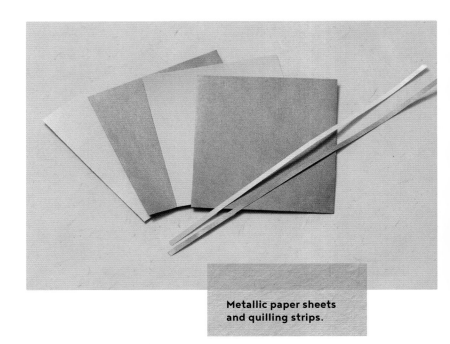

Metallic paper sheets and quilling strips.

Check Strip Edges

While metallic-edge quilling paper usually arrives in perfect condition from suppliers, it is possible to damage the evenly applied shine by striking the edge with a sharp tool or even a fingernail. Always check the metallic edge of strips to make sure the paint is unmarred before quilling, as skips may be noticeable in a finished piece.

Precut Strips

Whatever type of quilling strips you use, expect them to be accurately cut with a width that is exactly the same from end to end. If using archival supplies is important to you, buy strips that are labeled acid-free. Some paper brands are slightly heavier than others, and some colors are heavier within a single brand. Each type handles slightly differently, but all are cut with the grain to ensure smooth rolling. Quilling strips are usually reasonably priced, and it is fun to experiment with different brands to determine your favorites. Since I began quilling fifteen years ago, I have used many different types of strips from online suppliers in the United States and the United Kingdom. All have proven to be high-quality strips that are evenly cut and richly colored.

Metallic Quilling Strips

All of the projects in this book call for standard ⅛" (3 mm) wide strips with a gold, silver, or copper edge to give each piece the look of fine jewelry. While ⅛" (3 mm) may sound impossibly narrow, fear not! With practice, your fingers will grow accustomed to handling it fairly quickly.

The pendant and earring designs in this book are predominately made with metallic-edge black or ivory papers, but there is no need to limit yourself to just two choices. Metallic-edge papers can be ordered in a wide range of colors from at least three online retailers in the United States who import them from England. The British paper comes in packages of thirty ⅛"× 17" (3 mm × 43 cm) strips, which is enough to make several pieces of jewelry. Additionally, Dutch metallic-edge strips measuring ⅛" × 19½" (3 mm × 49.5 cm) are also available through a U.S. supplier and come twenty-five to a package.

If you want the look of metallic-edge strips but prefer a more subtle shine, try A Touch of Gold and A Touch of Silver quilling paper. This type of American-made metallic-edge strip is available in single color packages of fifty ⅛" × 24" (3 mm × 61 cm) strips, as well as packs of 100 multicolor ⅛" × 20-24" (3 mm × 51-61 cm) strips.

Colorful Quilling Strips

If you don't want a metallic edge, a wide array of precut color-saturated strips are available in widths both narrower and wider than ⅛" (3 mm). The thinnest width, frequently referred to simply as "narrow," is slightly wider than 1⁄16" (2 mm). There are also ¼" (6 mm), ⅜" (1.5 cm), ½" (1.3 cm), and ⅝" (1.6 cm) widths. You can choose from pearlized, metallic, glistening, parchment,

and vellum strips. There are even Holofoil-edge strips, mirror foil strips, strips with graduated colors that transition from dark to light along the length of the strip, and strips with a dark center and a color fade toward the ends. Yet another option is two-tone strips with different colors on each side. Your jewelry can be as colorful and diminutive or as big and bold as you like!

Paper Sheets

Many kinds of quilling papers are also available in sheet form if you prefer to cut your own strips with a paper trimmer or a rotary cutter on a self-healing cutting mat. In fact, metallic sheet paper can be cut into strips and is mentioned in several projects in this book as a quilling strip alternative for making paper bails, which are used to connect pendants to chains without the use of a jump ring. Keep in mind, however, that hand-cut strips will not have a shiny metallic edge, unless you apply one with ink or paint.

Gild Your Own Strips

In lieu of ordering gilded-edge paper, it is possible to create your own metallic-edge strips by pressing the rolled edge of coils against a silver, gold, or copper ink pad. The result is a slightly gilded effect, not the bright shine of purchased metallic-edge strips. Alternatively, use a small paintbrush or your finger-tip to lightly dab one edge of a strip with metallic acrylic paint. Allow it to dry before rolling.

Paper Storage

Keep your strips in a dry, dust-free place and away from sunlight to prevent fading. It is helpful to organize colors by brand name and number and store them in their original packaging, usually a clear plastic bag, so you can easily replenish your supply. Always a string saver, I'm in the habit of looking over any quilling paper scraps before sweeping them into the wastebasket. Because jewelry projects use lengths of metallic-edge paper that are as short as 1" (2.5 cm), it is worth keeping even the tiniest pieces. I store these bits in the corresponding bag of full-length strips.

Tools & Supplies

QUILLING TOOLS

These are the types of tools on which quilling strips are rolled.

L to R: Needle tool, paper-piercing tool, stiff wire, cake tester, Japanese superfine slotted tool, Savvy Slotted Tool, standard slotted tool, ultrafine slotted tool.

Needle Tool

With this tool, a strip is rolled around a needle. It takes a bit of extra effort to learn to quill with a needle tool, but the advantage is that it produces a coil with a tiny, perfectly round center. The disadvantage is that it takes more time to learn to quill with a needle tool, but with practice, you can become a pro at rolling smooth, even coils.

Needle Tool Substitutes

Any slim, sturdy wire can take the place of a needle tool. In fact, my first quilling tool was a cake tester, a stiff wire that is inserted into a cake to see if the batter is baked all the way through. A cocktail stick (round toothpick), a doll-making or upholstery needle, or even a corsage or hat pin can be substituted as well. Of course, a true needle tool with a handle will be more comfortable to grip, but these stand-ins will give you the opportunity to try your hand at needle-tool rolling.

Slotted Tool

With the easy-to-use slotted tool, a paper strip is slid into a slot that immediately grips the end, allowing for the smooth rotation of the tool with a relaxed hand. The trade-off is that the slot leaves a small crimp in the center of the coil. It's certainly

Coils made with different tools. L to R: Japanese superfine slotted tool, standard slotted tool, needle tool.

Finger Rolling *Quilling has a contingent of finger-rolling enthusiasts so that is always an option, too! Yes, some people prefer to quill without any tool at all, not only because of the convenience, but because the result is a coil without a noticeable center.*

not the end of the world, but sometimes a crimp is frowned upon by quilling purists. That said, I have yet to meet anyone who upon seeing a piece of slotted-tool jewelry for the first time is dismayed by the coil crimps. Instead, they are too busy exclaiming they can't believe the beautiful object is made of paper! I suggest learning to quill with both tools to determine your preference.

Slotted Tool Choices

It is important to note that not all slotted tools are alike. The standard slotted tool is a strong workhorse, but it leaves a considerably larger crimp than a fine slotted tool. A Japanese superfine slotted tool has a very small slot and a shaft that rotates smoothly. The crimp it produces can barely be detected. Common sense will tell you to not overstress the fine prongs by rolling the paper so tightly that the crimp is torn off, a practice some quillers employ with success when using a standard slotted tool. A tool called the

Savvy Slotted Tool is similar in design to the Japanese tool, but it has an ergonomic handle and the slot produces a slightly larger crimp. A fourth type of slotted tool has an ultrafine slot that is not set close to the handle, making it difficult to gain rolling leverage. That said, if it is the only tool you have access to as a new quiller, you may learn to quill beautifully with it.

Dowels

Dowels, or pegs, are used to shape various ring-coil types and sizes. You will notice throughout the book that project instructions list the diameter of the dowel used for making a particular ring coil.

If you prefer the convenience of professionally made dowels in graduated sizes, bamboo forms in a numbered set can be purchased from online quilling suppliers. Also available is a kit to make your own stacked dowel forms using quilling strips, as well as a plastic tool with an interchangeable handle with

which you can create uniform circular, square, and triangular ring coils. Jewelry makers may have a set of metal mandrels on hand that are ordinarily used for wire wrapping, but they are also useful for rolling paper-ring coils. Since time is precious, these options will save on rummaging around the house to find objects that are just the right size for your intended shapes.

On the other hand, it is cost-effective to improvise dowels with items you already have. I've used everything from craft-tool handles, pens and pencils, orangewood sticks, crochet hooks, and knitting needles to glue tubes, shampoo bottles, and even a hollow-handled medicine spoon. There is some room for minor size adjustments within these projects, so the components do not need to be made in the exact measurements as stated. Choose dowel substitutes as best you can. It can be helpful to keep a chart on which you note the diameter of a makeshift dowel so you can quickly reach for it when a new project calls for that particular size.

Additional Tools & Supplies

I mentioned that my first tool–a cake tester–was rudimentary at best, but it worked well enough to convince me that I could successfully twirl paper. I then headed straight to the paper-crafting aisle of my local craft store where I found a few quilling supplies. A kit for making quilled gift tags caught my eye, as well as what I thought was a needle tool, simply packaged in an unlabeled bag. I later learned it was a paper-piercing tool, also known as a clay-sculpting tool, that has a thicker shaft than a typical needle tool. Some things happen for a reason, though, as I soon came to think of it as a lucky accidental purchase. It is indispensable, always by my side as a useful tool for positioning coils, applying glue, and rolling ring coils around the handle or tip.

JEWELRY-MAKING SUPPLIES

Jewelry findings and tools are available at your local craft store. For the projects in this book, you will need:

- 2 pairs of flat-nose or chain-nose jewelry pliers for opening and closing jump rings

- Package of metal jump rings in assorted sizes for connecting quilled jewelry pieces to necklace chains or ear wires

- Ear wires

- Necklace chains in assorted lengths

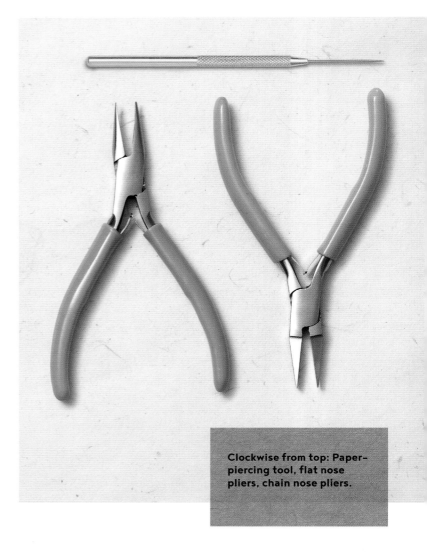

Clockwise from top: Paper-piercing tool, flat nose pliers, chain nose pliers.

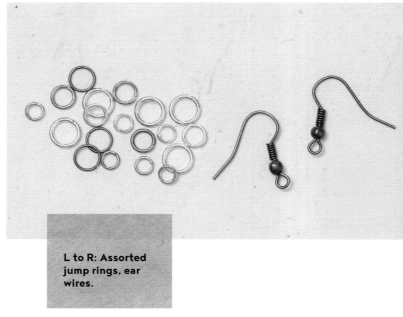

L to R: Assorted jump rings, ear wires.

ADDITIONAL TOOLS

You'll need a few more essentials, which you may already have on hand:

■ Fine-tip tweezers for ease in picking up tiny coils

■ Small, sharp detail scissors for trimming strip ends

■ 6" (15 cm) or 12" (30.5 cm) ruler

■ Pin assortment with various size heads useful for shaping domed tight coils

■ Lint-free damp cloth or paper towel, essential for moistening fingertips, keeping hands and work surface free of sticky glue, and for wiping excess glue from quilling strips

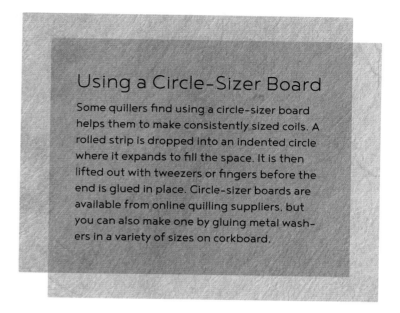

Using a Circle-Sizer Board

Some quillers find using a circle-sizer board helps them to make consistently sized coils. A rolled strip is dropped into an indented circle where it expands to fill the space. It is then lifted out with tweezers or fingers before the end is glued in place. Circle-sizer boards are available from online quilling suppliers, but you can also make one by gluing metal washers in a variety of sizes on corkboard.

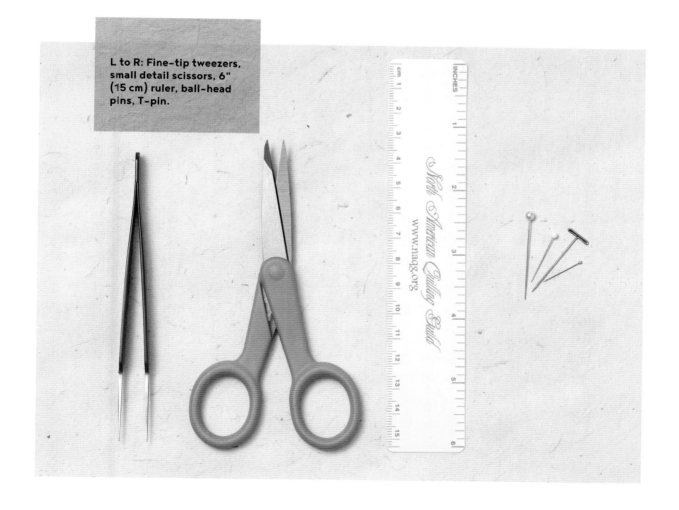

L to R: Fine-tip tweezers, small detail scissors, 6" (15 cm) ruler, ball-head pins, T-pin.

Glues & Fixatives

BEST GLUES FOR QUILLING

White Glue versus Clear Glue

Ask ten quillers to name their glue of choice and you'll likely get ten different answers. Elmer's School Glue, Aleene's Original Tacky Glue, and Sobo Premium Craft and Fabric Glue are names of white glues you'll frequently hear. I prefer to use a clear glue, such as Martha Stewart Crafts All-Purpose Gel Adhesive. (Elmer's Clear School Glue is another option.) Unlike white glue, clear glues do not quickly thicken and develop a skin when exposed to air on a glue palette.

safety note: *I always look for glues and fixatives that are nontoxic and free of fumes.*

Acid-Free Glue

Acidic glues can discolor paper and cause it to become brittle over time, so I prefer to use glues that are acid-free. Martha Stewart Crafts All-Purpose Gel Adhesive is an example of an acid-free clear glue. Aleene's makes an acid-free white Tacky Glue.

Adhering to Metal or Plastic

When gluing quilled pieces to a nonporous surface, such as metal or plastic, Crafter's Pick The Ultimate is my adhesive of choice because it securely holds coils and scrolls in place, dries clear, and is durable and nontoxic.

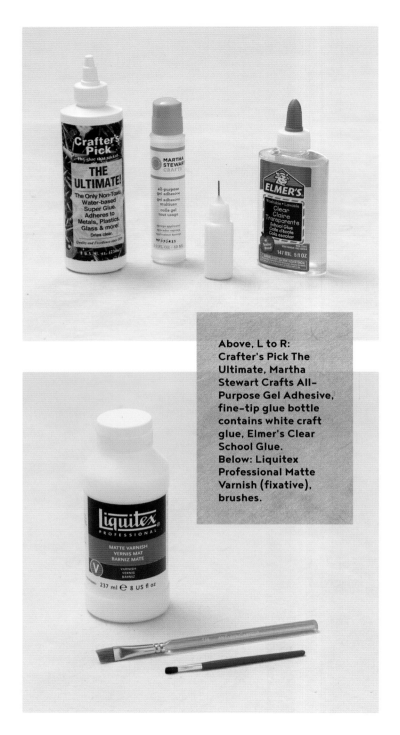

Above, L to R: Crafter's Pick The Ultimate, Martha Stewart Crafts All-Purpose Gel Adhesive, fine-tip glue bottle contains white craft glue, Elmer's Clear School Glue. Below: Liquitex Professional Matte Varnish (fixative), brushes.

I prefer to place a small dollop of glue on a palette (a recycled plastic container lid works really well) and dip from it sparingly with the tip of a ball-head pin, paper-piercing tool, or T-pin. This way, I can easily control the amount of glue I use and keep my hand relaxed, because there is no squeezing motion as there is with a plastic bottle.

FIXATIVES

Truth be told, I rarely use a fixative on quilled jewelry. I prefer the look of natural paper rather than the plastic shine of glossy fixatives, not to mention there is always the chance that moisture in a spray or brush-on product will cause coil centers to swell. However, for an extra layer of protection, especially if you live in a warm, humid climate, you can apply a protective coating, such as Liquitex Professional Matte Varnish. (Apply a thin layer or two using a small paintbrush or repurposed makeup brush.) This type of varnish is nontoxic, virtually odor-free, and will not significantly change the look of quilling paper. I recommend applying it only to the back of a jewelry piece because it will dull the bright shine of metallic-edge paper.

Caring for and Storing Quilled Jewelry

Because I'm careful to wear quilled jewelry gently on a chain around my neck or dangling from my earlobes, I find that simple glue is sufficient to create a long-lasting piece. I always tell recipients of my paper pendants and earrings to treat them as they would any fine jewelry: last thing on, first thing off, and never take them for a swim.

Store quilled jewelry carefully as well. I recommend placing it flat in a small box or ziplock plastic bag inside a cool, non-humid, and dust-free place, such as a drawer or jewelry box. Doing so will also help to delay the tarnishing of sterling silver jump rings and ear wires. You may wish to wrap the necklace chain or ear wires in tissue to prevent them from pressing against the metallic surface and possibly damaging them.

When traveling, similarly protect a quilled-jewelry piece by packaging it separately in a sturdy box, such as a small mint tin, before placing it in your suitcase.

Storing Glue During Use

For convenience, many quillers decant white craft glue into a soft plastic squeeze bottle with a fine-tip applicator. They position the bottle upside down in a votive candle holder or shot glass with the tip on a piece of damp cloth or paper towel to prevent the glue from hardening in the tip while they work.

CHAPTER TWO

Simply the Basics

I'm pretty sure most crafters remember the moment they discovered quilling—it has that effect on people! While flipping through the pages of a magazine, I was stopped in my tracks by a beautifully photographed article featuring an assortment of gracefully sculpted scrolls and coils. Paper, I remember thinking, can it be? I had been an avid crafter for several decades, but this was my first glimpse of rolled strips. How can thin paper be made to stand on edge? I knew immediately that I wanted to learn everything possible about this unusual and, at the time, relatively little-known technique. The thought crossed my mind that even though quilling appeared challenging to master, it would be worth it. Besides, the tools were so simple, surely I—or anyone—could learn to do it, too.

How to Use a Needle Tool & Slotted Tool

If your hands are dry, moisten fingertips on a damp cloth or paper towel before rolling a strip to increase your control of the paper. Also, trim the beginning and end of each strip so there is no glue residue. (A skein of strips is held together at the top and bottom with rubbery glue, similar to a notepad.)

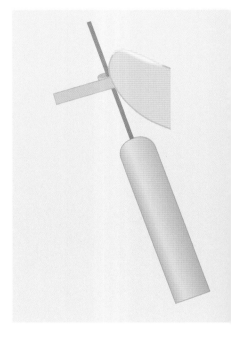

NEEDLE TOOL

1 Bend one end of a quilling strip around the tip of the needle.

2 Hold the tool handle steady in one hand and use the thumb and index finger of the other hand to roll the strip around the needle using light, even finger pressure.

3 When you reach the end of the strip, depending on its intended use, either maintain the tightly rolled coil by gluing the end while the strip is still on the needle or allow the strip to relax.

4 Slide the coil off the needle.

tip: *Be sure to rotate the paper, not the tool.*

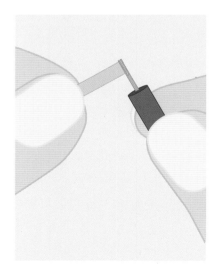

SLOTTED TOOL

1 Slide one end of a strip into the slot, taking care that it does not extend beyond the slot.

2 Turn the tool with one hand while evenly guiding the strip with the other. The strip will wind into a coil almost effortlessly.

3 When you reach the end of the strip, depending on its intended use, either maintain the tightly rolled coil by gluing the end while the strip is still on the tool or allow the strip to relax.

4 Slide the coil off the tool.

Hand Care

While I admire the look of the round center produced by a needle tool as compared to the slotted tool's crimp, I find that a needle tool places a fair amount of pressure on the thumb and index finger of my rolling hand. To avoid a repetitive stress injury, take breaks when using a needle tool. Resist gripping it more tightly than necessary and flex your hands periodically.

Determining the Best Strip Length

How do I know what strip length to use? This is a common question many new quillers ask. The instructions in this book indicate strip measurements, but they are only recommendations. The type of tool I use may be different than the one you use. Also, we might not apply the same amount of finger pressure while rolling a strip. My best advice is to practice rolling until your finger tension becomes consistent and your coils are uniform in size. Don't worry too much if your coils don't look exactly the same as the ones pictured here. As a beginner, your main goal is to achieve evenly rolled coils that lie flat. Once you have developed a smooth rolling ability, it will be time to focus on relaxing or tightening your finger tension to create a coil in the size you desire.

Remember, the goal is to create coils that look alike when rolled from the same strip length. Ideally, the inner rotations will be evenly distributed within the coil. The more loosely a strip is rolled, the larger the coil will be, and conversely, if more pressure is used, a coil will be smaller with compact inner rotations. With repetition, your skill will improve—nothing takes the place of practice. In time, you will discover the strip length that will produce the desired coil size. The key is to roll with even finger tension and your work will have a pleasing uniformity.

L to R: Needle tool teardrop coils made with 5" (12.5 cm), 4" (10 cm), and 3" (7.5 cm) strips.

Working With Strips

MAKING LONGER STRIPS

Butting Ends Together

When rolling a tight coil with multiple strips, a smooth result can be achieved by butting a bluntly cut strip end against the glued, bluntly cut end of the previously rolled strip **(Figure 1)**.

Gluing Strips Together Before Rolling

Another method is to join strips together before rolling to create a longer one. Simply tear one end of each strip, apply a small amount of glue to the torn ends **(Figure 2)**, and press to smoothly overlap them.

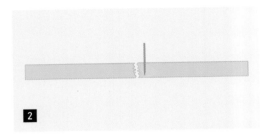

CREATING THICKER STRIPS

A few of the projects in this book, such as the Solitary Leaf Pendant and the Loops and Leaves Pendant, call for double- or even triple-thickness strips. To make a double-thickness strip, apply a thin, even coat of glue along the length of one strip and place a second strip on top of it. Repeat with a third strip **(Figure 3)**. Smooth the sturdy new strip between your fingers to press out any air bubbles. If necessary, lightly wipe a damp cloth or paper towel along both sides and the edges to remove excess glue. Trim strip ends neatly. Allow the strip to dry completely–patience is key here! The layers will separate and buckle if the glue is the least bit damp when rolling.

HANDLING THICKER STRIPS

Rolling thick strips requires more finger pressure than working with single strips. Before shaping this type of strip, run it over the handle of your needle tool or paper-piercing tool as if you were curling paper ribbon on the open blade of a pair of scissors **(Figure 4)**. This will help to soften the paper, making it easier to roll.

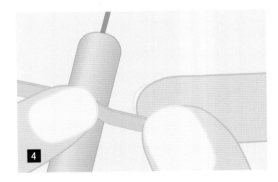

Gluing Techniques

GLUING QUILLED PIECES TOGETHER

When you have successfully made all of the coils and scrolls required for a project, glue them together on a nonstick work surface. You can use pins to hold each component in place while the glue dries **(Figure 1)**, but this is usually not necessary. An acrylic sheet, such as a page-protector sleeve or a piece of waxed paper placed over corkboard can serve as a work surface, as will something as simple as an upcycled Styrofoam tray. The use of a nonstick board is simply preventative. If you are careful to limit the amount of glue, and to glue coil to coil rather than coil to board, there will be no need to pop your project off the slick surface when the glue has dried.

In time, you will learn precisely how much glue is needed to sufficiently hold components together—usually far less than expected.

1

HIDING GLUE & STRIP ENDS

Ideally, your goal is a completed project on which no glue can be detected. Although most craft glues dry clear, they leave a shiny snail trail. To avoid this, use the smallest amount of glue possible. If you accidentally get a bit of glue on the outer edge of a coil, use a damp cloth or paper towel to quickly wipe it away before the glue dries.

tip: *Take time to position quilled components so the ends meet and are therefore hidden when the coils are glued together. It is tiny details like this that add up to a perfectly quilled design.*

Opening & Closing Jump Rings

With the split positioned at the top and holding a pair of flat-nose or chain-nose jewelry pliers in each hand, grasp each side of the split and twist open the jump ring **(Figure 1)**. Reverse the twisting motion to close the jump ring **(Figure 2)**.

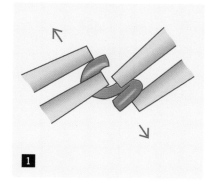

1

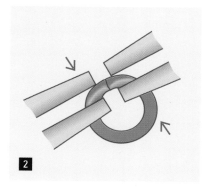

2

CHAPTER THREE

Making Coils & Scrolls

This chapter includes instructions for making a variety of scrolls and coils that are used in the projects in this book as well as a few bonus styles that you can work into your own designs. They are divided by technique into three sections: Scrolls, Coils (in which the paper is rolled, but not allowed to relax before the end is glued), and Relaxed Coils (in which the paper is rolled and allowed to relax before it is slipped off the tool, then pinched into shape and glued).

It is important to note that this is by no means a comprehensive guide of all quilling shapes or techniques. Instead, this chapter focuses on the coils and scrolls that are needed to make the projects in this book. Whether you are new to quilling or a seasoned veteran, I hope you will be inspired to make many beautiful pieces of modern paper jewelry.

The Difference Between Scrolls & Coils

While quilling might appear complicated at first glance because of the curving loops, the shapes are either scrolls or coils. The main difference between the two is that the end of a coil is glued in place, while most scrolls do not require glue. (An exception is the double scroll that has a glued tail.)

The Loose Scroll

THE BASIC BUILDING BLOCK OF QUILLING

When a rolled strip is slipped off a quilling tool and allowed to loosen or relax, it is referred to as a loose (or single) scroll—the basic building block of many quilled shapes. It is the loose scroll that is pinched and glued in a variety of ways to create a multitude of different coils, such as a closed loose coil, a teardrop coil, and a marquise coil.

note: *Despite its lacy appearance, a coiled strip of paper is quite a bit stronger than you might think. Press your thumb on a firmly rolled coil that has been placed on a flat surface and it will likely survive unscathed.*

Scrolls

LOOSE (OR SINGLE) SCROLL

Because the end of a loose scroll isn't glued, it has a curved tail. You can adjust the curve with your fingers and trim it as long or short as you like.

1 Roll a strip with bluntly cut ends around a quilling tool **(Figure 1)**.

2 Slip the coil off the tool and allow it to relax **(Figure 2)**.

3 Trim the length of the curved loose end as desired.

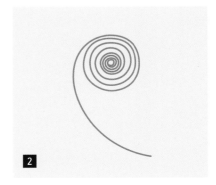

DOUBLE SCROLL

For the double scroll and flag scroll, you will need to use a needle tool or standard slotted tool because the slot of a fine-slotted tool is not wide enough to accommodate two strips at once.

1 Stack and roll 2 equal length strips with bluntly cut ends together on a quilling needle tool or standard slotted tool **(Figure 1)**.

2 Slip the double strip coil off the tool and allow it to relax.

3 Gently pull the strip ends apart to partially separate them **(Figure 2)**.

4 Glue the ends together where desired, depending on how large or small you want the double scroll to be **(Figure 3)**. The end of the inner scroll paper will be longer than the outer layer.

5 Trim the excess (longer) strip **(Figure 4)**.

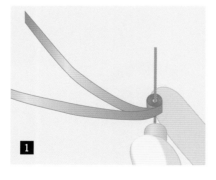

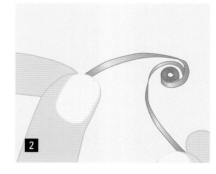

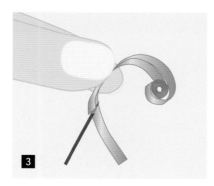

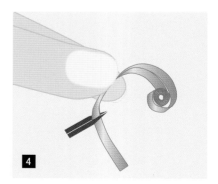

FLAG SCROLL

1 Fold a strip with bluntly cut ends in half **(Figure 1)**.

2 Roll the stacked ends together toward the fold on a needle tool or standard slotted tool. While rolling, the upper half of the strip will bulge outward and the lower half will remain straight **(Figure 2)**.

3 Stop rolling where desired and slip the scroll off the tool.

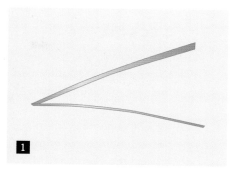

HEART SCROLL

1 Fold a strip with bluntly cut ends in half.

2 Roll one end around a slotted tool or needle tool to the midpoint **(Figure 1)**.

3 Roll the other end of the strip to the midpoint and slip the scroll off the tool **(Figure 2)**.

4 Apply a tiny amount of glue between the coils to maintain their position, if desired.

S SCROLL

Before rolling, you may want to use a pencil to lightly mark the strip midpoint **(Figure 1)**.

1 Roll one end of a strip with bluntly cut ends toward the center and slip the strip off the tool.

2 Turn the strip over and roll the opposite end toward the strip center **(Figure 2)**.

3 Adjust the distance between the coils by gently pulling them apart to create an S scroll with equally sized ends **(Figure 3)**.

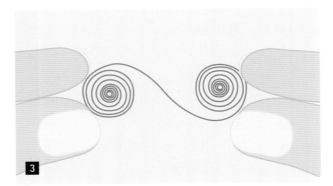

Coils

Whether you should begin rolling a coil with a bluntly cut or torn end depends on the type and size of the coil. For example, it doesn't matter for a small tight coil because the end will barely be visible, but inside a teardrop coil, a torn end can look a bit messy. When I make a tight coil, closed loose coil, or a ring coil, I tear the far end of the strip because a torn end blends more smoothly when glued. Therefore, the coil will look as round as possible.

tip: *At times it will be necessary to glue the starting end of a strip in place inside a coil. To do this, use a pin to apply a tiny amount of glue from the back (non-gilded) side to avoid scratching the metallic surface.*

TIGHT COIL

1 Roll a strip with a torn far end on a needle or slotted tool.

2 Glue the torn end while the coil is still on the tool without allowing the strip to relax **(Figure 1)**.

3 Slide the coil off the tool **(Figure 2)**.

DOMED TIGHT COIL

1 Make a tight coil.

2 Press the ball head of a pin against one flat side of the coil to create a curved top or dome **(Figure 1)**.

3 Apply a coating of glue on the inside of the dome with the tip of a pin or paper-piercing tool to preserve the curve **(Figure 2)**.

OVAL DOMED TIGHT COIL

1 Make a domed tight coil, but do not apply glue inside the dome.

2 Gently pinch 2 opposite points of the coil with your thumb and index finger or with a pair of tweezers **(Figure 3)** to create an oval shape **(Figure 4)**.

3 Apply glue inside the oval dome.

Domed Tight Coils and Oval Domed Tight Coils.

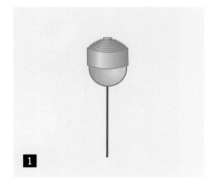

RING COIL

1 Roll a strip with torn ends around a dowel or a cylindrical object, such as a quilling-tool handle or glue bottle **(Figure 1)**.

2 Glue the torn end while the coil is still on the dowel **(Figure 2)** or slip the coil off the dowel and glue the ends **(Figure 3)**. (Try gluing the end both ways to see which technique you prefer.)

3 Glue the interior end in place **(Figure 4)**.

tip : *Roll a ring coil using even finger pressure on the paper—neither too firmly or loosely—as you will need to slip it off the dowel.*

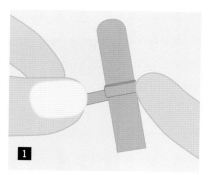

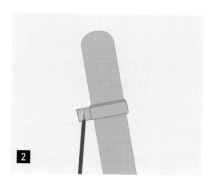

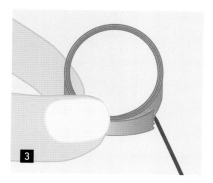

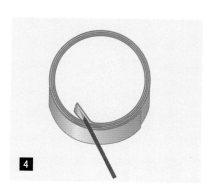

OVAL RING COIL

1 Make a Ring Coil.

2 Compress the coil gently between your thumb and index finger to form an oval **(Figure 1)**.

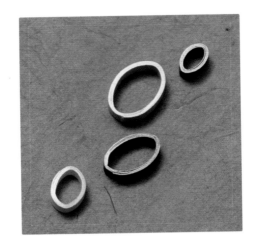

TEARDROP RING COIL

1 Roll a strip with bluntly cut ends around a dowel.

2 Slip the coil off the dowel and pinch a point close to the interior strip end (the starting point) **(Figure 1)**.

3 Glue the strip end at the point and trim the excess paper **(Figure 2)**.

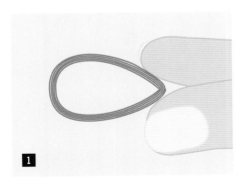

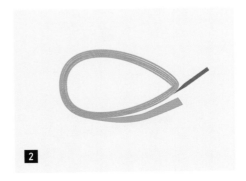

MARQUISE RING COIL

1 Roll a strip with bluntly cut ends around a dowel.

2 Slip the coil off the dowel. Pinch a point close to the interior strip end and at the opposite side to create 2 points **(Figure 1)**.

3 Glue the end at a point and trim the excess strip **(Figure 2)**.

4 As with all Ring Coil shapes, glue the interior end in place.

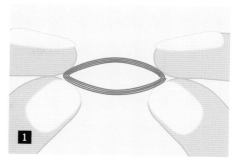

These stunning Shooting Star Earrings are made with two sizes of marquise ring coils, a teardrop ring coil, and a domed tight coil.

TRIANGLE RING COIL

1 Roll a strip with bluntly cut ends around a dowel.

2 Slip the coil off the dowel and pinch a point close to the interior strip end to create a teardrop shape **(Figure 1)**.

3 Pinch the curved portion 2 more times where desired, creating a triangle **(Figure 2)**.

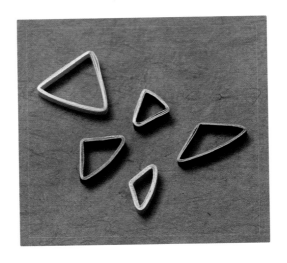

4 Glue the end at a point and trim the excess strip.

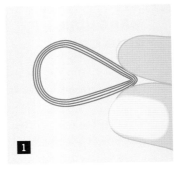

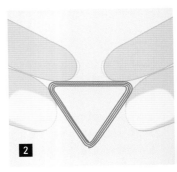

SQUARE RING COIL

1 Roll a strip with bluntly cut ends around a dowel.

2 Slip the coil off the dowel. Pinch a point close to the interior strip end and at the opposite side to create a marquise shape **(Figure 1)**.

3 Rotate the marquise 90 degrees and pinch at 2 more opposite points to create a square ring coil **(Figure 2)**.

4 Glue the end at a point and trim the excess strip.

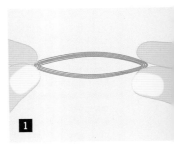

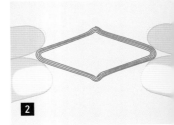

RECTANGLE RING COIL

1 Roll a strip with bluntly cut ends around a dowel.

2 Slip the coil off the dowel. Pinch a point close to the interior strip end and also at an opposite point to create a marquise ring coil (**Figure 1**).

3 Rotate the marquise 45 degrees and pinch at 2 more opposite points to create a rectangle ring coil (**Figure 2**).

4 Glue the end at a point and trim the excess strip.

note: Because rectangles can vary in depth, you may prefer to rotate the marquise less or more than 45 degrees to create a shallower or deeper rectangle.

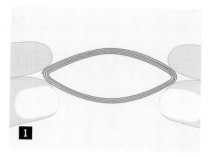

This Swirled Scrolls Pendant features a square ring coil that contains single and double scrolls.

Relaxed Coils

Relaxed coils are strips that are rolled on a quilling tool and allowed to naturally unwind before being slipped off the tool.

CLOSED LOOSE COIL

1 Roll a strip on a quilling tool to create a coil **(Figure 1)**.

2 Allow the coil to relax **(Figure 2)**.

3 Slip the coil off the tool and glue the torn end **(Figure 3)**.

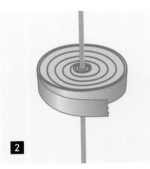

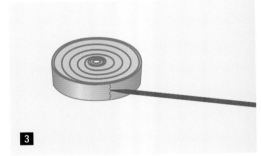

Perfecting Inner Coils

If your loose coils don't spring open evenly, use a ball-head pin to jiggle the inner rotations, evenly spacing them before pinching and gluing. This isn't always necessary, but it can be quite the time-saver because it takes the place of rerolling a coil to achieve even expansion. Another tip is to gently huff on a coil—your warm, moist breath will help it expand.

TEARDROP COIL

1 Roll a strip on a quilling tool. Allow the coil to relax and slip it off the tool **(Figure 1)**.

2 Pinch the coil near the end of the strip **(Figure 2)**.

3 If desired, use a pin to first pull the center toward one side of the coil and then evenly space the inner coil rotations with the pin before pinching the point **(Figure 3)**.

4 Glue the end **(Figure 4)**. Trim the excess paper **(Figure 5)**.

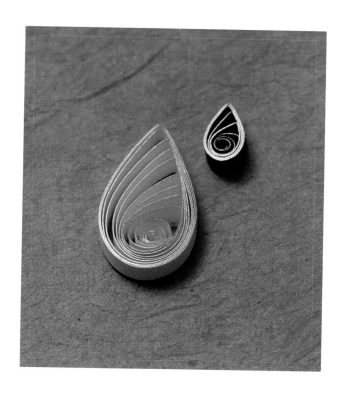

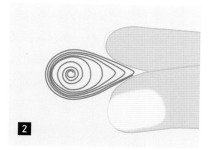

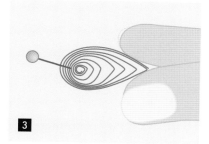

SHAPED TEARDROP COIL

1 Make a Teardrop Coil.

2 Hold the rounded end with the thumb and index finger of one hand. Gently curve the point with the thumb and index finger of your other hand (**Figure 1**).

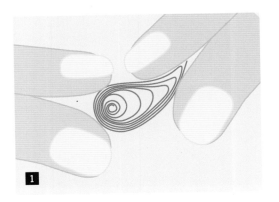

MARQUISE COIL

1 Make a Loose Coil and slip it off the tool (**Figure 1**).

2 Pinch a point close to the exterior strip end and on the opposite side to create 2 points (**Figure 2**). If needed, use a straight pin to adjust the inner coils so the coil center is positioned in the middle of the marquise before pinching.

3 Glue the end and trim the excess paper.

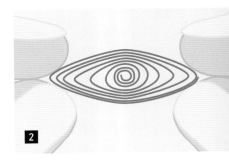

SHAPED MARQUISE COIL

1 Make a Marquise Coil.

2 Grasp each point with a thumb and index finger. Gently curve one point upward and the other point downward **(Figure 1)**.

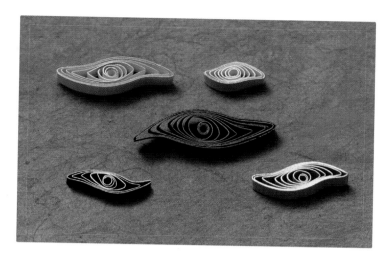

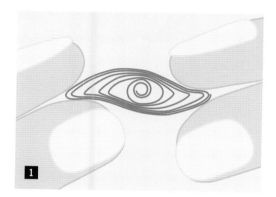

This detailed Double Ring Pendant features clusters of shaped marquise coils.

CHAPTER FOUR

Projects

———

Now that you are familiar with the quilling
technique and have practiced rolling each
kind of coil and scroll, it is time to make
jewelry! To keep things simple, standard-
width ⅛" (3 mm) quilling strips are used for
all of the projects in this book except in a few
instances where a slightly narrower strip is
noted. My best advice is to work slowly, use a
light touch, and enjoy the process. Like any
good thing, quilling simply can't be rushed.

FINISHED SIZE
Each earring
measures 1⅛" × 1⅛"
(2.8 cm × 2.8 cm).

SHAPES USED
Marquise ring coil

Domed tight coil

Teardrop ring coil

MATERIALS
Black with silver edge
quilling paper

2 silver-tone 5 mm
jump rings

2 silver-tone 4 mm
jump rings

2 silver-tone ear wires

TOOLS
Glue

Small scissors

Ruler

Fine-tip tweezers

Ball-head pins

Paper-piercing tool

½" (1.3 cm) dowel

¼" (6 mm) dowel

⅛" (3 mm) or slightly
larger dowel

Nonstick work board

Plastic lid or fine-tip
glue bottle

Damp cloth or
paper towel

2 pairs of flat-nose or
chain-nose jewelry pliers

Fixative (optional)

Watercolor brush
(optional)

Shooting Star EARRINGS

A stylish play on a traditional quilled flower,
all eyes will be on you when you wear these
showstopping earrings composed of simple
marquise ring coils arranged around a domed
tight coil. Make the companion Celestial Flower
Pendant, too.

FOR EACH EARRING:

1 Roll a 6" (15 cm) strip around a ½" (1.3 cm) dowel. Hold the ring coil firmly so it does not loosen and slip it off the dowel. Pinch the ring coil close to where the strip began and directly opposite it to make a marquise ring coil **(Figure 1)**. Glue the end and trim the excess paper. Use a pin to apply a tiny amount of glue under the cut end inside the coil. Make 3 marquise ring coils total for the large petals.

2 Roll a 3½" (9 cm) strip around a ¼" (6 mm) dowel. Complete in the same manner as step 1 to make a marquise ring coil. Make 3 marquise ring coils total for the small petals.

3 Make a domed tight coil for the flower center by rolling a 3" (7.5 cm) strip with a quilling tool **(Figure 2)**. Glue the torn end and press a ball-head pin against one flat side of the coil to create a dome. Apply a bit of glue inside the dome with the tip of a pin or paper-piercing tool to preserve the curve.

4 Roll a 2½" (6.5 cm) strip around a ⅛" (3 mm) or slightly larger dowel. Slide the coil off the dowel and pinch one point to create a teardrop ring coil. Glue the end and trim the excess paper at the point.

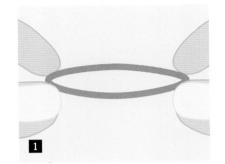

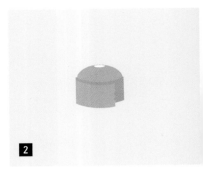

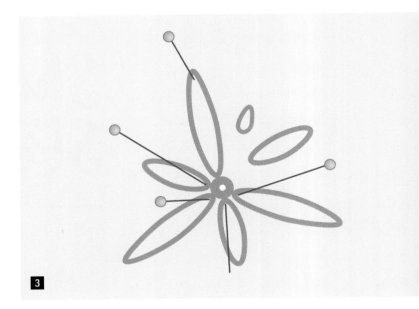

5 Referring to **Figure 3**, arrange the petals evenly around the flower center, alternating large and small sizes as shown. Position the teardrop ring coil between a large and small petal. Work on a nonstick work board and use pins to hold the coils in place while gluing, if desired.

6 When the glue has dried enough to handle the earring, remove the pins. Turn the earring over and apply a small dot of glue with the tip of a pin

or paper-piercing tool on each join to reinforce it **(Figure 4)**. Allow the glue to dry completely.

7 Brush a thin coating of fixative onto the non-metallic side of the earring, if desired. Allow the glue and fixative to dry completely, preferably overnight.

8 Use 2 pairs of jewelry pliers to twist open a 5 mm jump ring. Slip the jump ring through the teardrop ring coil and reverse the twisting motion to

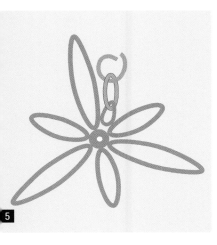

lose the jump ring. In the same
anner, open a 4 mm jump ring
nd slip it onto the 5 mm jump
ng **(Figure 5)**.

Slip an earring wire onto the
4 mm jump ring and close
e jump ring **(Figure 6)**.

FINISHED SIZE

Pendant measures 1⅛"
× 2⅛" (2.8 cm × 5.3 cm).

SHAPES USED

Modified ring coil

Marquise ring coil

Domed tight coil

MATERIALS

Ivory with gold edge
quilling paper

Pearlized gold quilling
paper (for the bail)

Necklace of choice

TOOLS

Quilling tool

Glue

Small scissors

Ruler

Fine-tip tweezers

Ball-head pins

Paper-piercing tool

1¼" (3.2 cm) dowel

½" (1.3 cm) dowel

¼" (6 mm) dowel

⅜" (1 cm) dowel

Nonstick work board

Plastic lid or fine-tip
glue bottle

Damp cloth or
paper towel

Fixative (optional)

Watercolor brush
(optional)

Celestial Flower PENDANT

If you enjoy wearing matching jewelry, this heavenly pendant pairs perfectly with the Shooting Star Earrings. Although it will draw rave reviews when worn solo, too!

1 Roll a 17" (43 cm) strip with bluntly cut ends around a 1¼" (3.2 cm) dowel to create a large ring coil. Be sure to roll the strip firmly, but keep it loose enough to slip the unglued coil off the dowel.

tip: *To keep the strip firmly wound, you can apply tiny dots of glue on the quilling strip as you roll the ring coil* **(Figure 1).**

2 Slip the ring coil off the dowel and pinch the coil close to the initial cut end. Glue the end and trim the excess paper. Apply a tiny amount of glue with a pin to the cut end inside the coil to hold it in place **(Figure 2).**

3 Make another pinch about one index-finger width away from the first pinched closure, indenting the space between them to create a recessed curve that is about ½" (1.3 cm) wide **(Figure 3).**

4 Gently pinch the bottom of the coil to a rounded point **(Figure 4)**. Brush a thin coating of fixative on the reverse side, if desired. Set the pendant frame aside to dry.

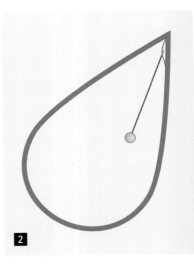
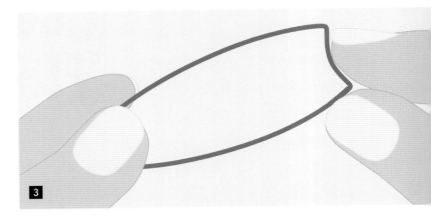

5 Roll a 6" (15 cm) strip around a ½" (1.3 cm) dowel. Hold the coil firmly so it does not loosen and slide it off the dowel. Pinch a point close to the interior strip end and on the opposite side to create a marquise ring coil. Glue the end and trim the excess paper. Apply a tiny amount of glue to the cut end inside the coil to hold it in place. Make 3 marquise ring coils total for the large petals.

6 Roll a 3½" (9 cm) strip around a ¼" (6 mm) dowel. Complete in the same manner as the large petals. Make 3 small marquise shapes total for the small petals.

7 Roll a 3" (7.5 cm) strip on a quilling tool to make a domed tight coil for the flower center. Glue the torn end and press a ball-head pin against one flat side of the coil to create a dome. Apply a bit of glue inside the dome with the tip of a pin or paper-piercing tool to preserve the curve.

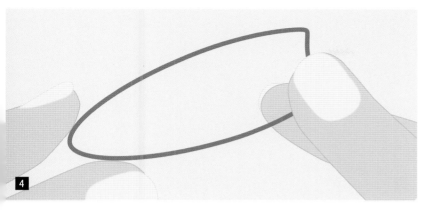

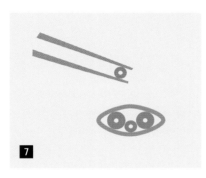

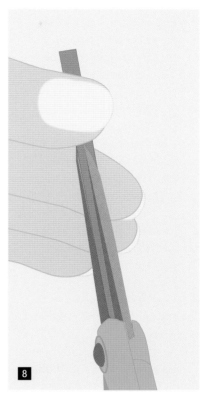

8 Assemble the flower components on a nonstick work board **(Figure 5)**, using pins to hold them in place, if desired. Glue the petals evenly around the flower center, alternating large and small sizes.

9 Make a marquise ring coil by rolling a 4" (10 cm) strip around a ⅜" (1 cm) dowel. Complete the marquise shape in the same manner as step 5.

10 Make 4 domed tight coils using two 1¼" (3.2 cm) strips and two 2" (5 cm) strips **(Figure 6)**.

11 Glue the domed tight coils inside the marquise ring coil with the 2" (5 cm) coils on opposite sides and the 1¼" (3.2 cm) coils sandwiched vertically between them **(Figure 7)**.

---

tip: *Tweezers are invaluable when handling such tiny coils.*

---

12 Make a metallic-paper jump ring: Trim the width of a ⅛" × 3" (3 mm × 7.5 cm) strip of pearlized gold quilling paper so that it is slightly narrower than (3 mm) **(Figure 8)**. (This gives a finer look in proportion to the scale of the pendant.)

Fold down one end of the strip about ¼" (6 mm) **(Figure 9)** and wrap the strip around the initial fold 4 times **(Firgure 10)**. Glue the end and trim the excess paper. Apply a tiny amount of glue to the strip end inside the coil to hold it in place.

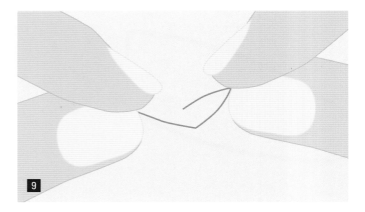

13 Referring to **Figure 11**, arrange the pendant components on a nonstick work board as shown, using pins if desired. Glue the pieces together in the following order:

a. Glue the marquise ring coil horizontally on the pendant outline indentation.

b. Glue the metallic-paper bail to the top center of the marquise ring coil.

c. Apply dots of glue to the back of the flower and glue it to the front edges of the pendant outline.

14 When the glue has dried enough to handle the pendant, turn it over and apply a small dot of glue with the tip of a pin or paper-piercing tool on each join as reinforcement. Allow the glue to dry completely, preferably overnight.

15 Slide a necklace chain through the metallic-paper bail.

Applying a bit of glue to each spot where the flower meets the frame on the back of the pendant will make the design extra sturdy.

FINISHED SIZE
Each earring
measures $5/16$" × $1\frac{3}{8}$"
(8 mm × 3.5 cm).

SHAPES USED
Teardrop ring coil

Oval ring coil

Domed tight coil

MATERIALS
Black with gold edge
quilling paper

Black with silver edge
quilling paper

2 silver-tone 5 mm
jump rings

2 silver -tone 4 mm
jump rings

2 silver-tone ear wires

TOOLS
Quilling tool

Glue

Small scissors

Ruler

Fine-tip tweezers

Ball-head pins

Paper-piercing tool

¼" (6 mm) dowel

Nonstick work board

Plastic lid or fine-tip
glue bottle

Damp cloth or
paper towel

2 pairs of flat-nose or
chain-nose jewelry pliers

Fixative (optional)

Watercolor brush
(optional)

Modern Hardware

EARRINGS

These mixed-metal ring-coil earrings are quite easy to make and lighter than air to wear. They look great paired with a chic black dress.

FOR EACH EARRING:

1 Roll a 6½" (16.5 cm) black with silver edge strip around a ¼" (6 mm) dowel. Slip the coil off the tool and pinch where the cut end of the strip is visible inside the ring coil to create a teardrop ring coil. Glue the strip at this point and trim the excess paper. Apply a tiny amount of glue under the cut end inside the coil to hold it in place. Make 2 teardrop ring coils total **(Figure 1)**.

2 Roll a 6½" (16.5 cm) black with silver edge strip with torn ends around the same size dowel. Glue the end in place, slip the coil off the tool, and compress it gently between fingers or with tweezers to create an oval **(Figure 2)**. Apply a tiny amount of glue under the loose end inside the coil to hold it in place.

3 Roll a 1¼" (3.8 cm) black with gold edge strip on a needle or slotted tool to make a domed tight coil. Glue the torn end and press a ball head pin against one flat side of the coil to create a dome. Apply a bit of glue inside the dome with the tip of a pin or paper piercing tool to preserve the curve. Make 5 domed tight coils total **(Figure 3)**.

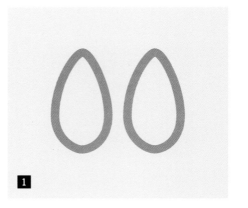

4 Glue the quilled components together on a nonstick work board, using pins if desired **(Figure 4)**.

5 When the glue has dried enough to handle the earrings, remove the pins, turn the earrings over, and dot glue onto all joins with the tip of a pin or paper-piercing tool. Brush a thin coating of fixative on the earring backs to strengthen the paper, if desired. Allow the glue and fixative to dry completely, preferably overnight.

6 Use 2 pairs of jewelry pliers to twist open a 5 mm jump ring and slip it through the top teardrop ring coil. Reverse the twisting motion to close the jump ring. Open a 4 mm jump ring in the same manner and slip it through the first jump ring, then slip on an ear wire. Close the second jump ring.

FINISHED SIZE
Pendant measures
1¼" × 1½" (3.2 cm
× 3.8 cm).

SHAPES USED
Ring coil

Tight coil

Domed tight coil

MATERIALS
Blue with silver edge
quilling paper

Silver-tone 7 mm
jump ring

Silver-tone necklace
chain of choice

TOOLS
Quilling tool

Glue

Small scissors

Ruler

Fine-tip tweezers

Ball-head pins

Paper-piercing tool

⅛" (1 cm) dowel

¼" (6 mm) dowel

Nonstick work board

Plastic lid or fine-tip glue
bottle

Damp cloth or
paper towel

2 pairs of flat-nose or
chain-nose jewelry
pliers

Fixative (optional)

Watercolor brush
(optional)

Blue Bubbles

PENDANT

—

While all of the other projects in this book are a
mix of ivory and black quilling paper with a silver,
gold, or copper edge, I chose blue with silver to
make this pendant, as the colors make me think
of a summer day spent at a water park. This is a
good project for beginners because there is no
need to exactly replicate coil sizes or positions.
The free-form design will attract admiring
glances no matter how the bubbles are sized and
arranged.

note: For the ring coils in this project, both ends of the strip should be torn. Because a torn end is less noticeable than a bluntly cut end on a ring coil, the outer and inner surfaces will appear smooth and round.

1 To create the largest ring coil, roll an 11" (28 cm) strip with torn ends around a ³⁄₈" (1 cm) dowel **(Figure 1)**. Glue the end. Apply a tiny amount of glue to the torn end inside the coil to hold it in place. Make 3 ring coils.

2 Roll a 6" (15 cm) strip with torn ends around a ¼" (6 mm) dowel to create a smaller ring coil **(Figure 2)**. Glue both ends in the same manner as step 1. Make 5 ring coils total.

3 Make 6 tight coils using 3" (7.5 cm) strips and gluing the torn ends.

tip: A slotted tool is recommended for making tight coils because the slot grips the strip, making it easy to wind.

Place the tight coils, gilded side down, on a tabletop and gently roll across each one a few times with the handle of a tool or tap them with a flat object to smooth the surface, if needed **(Figure 3)**.

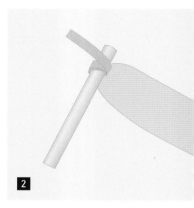

4 Roll a 3" (7.5 cm) strip on the tip of a paper-piercing tool or cocktail stick (round toothpick) to create a tight coil with a center hole large enough to accommodate a jump ring **(Figure 4)**. Glue the torn end. Press against the gilded edge with a ball-head pin to create a non-gilded, blue domed tight coil **(Figure 5)**. Apply a tiny amount of glue inside the dome to preserve the curve. Repeat this step to create 6 domed ring coils total.

5

6

7

tip : *When gluing components together in any quilled design, always position a glued end against an adjoining coil so the seam is hidden. This gives a neat appearance.*

6 When the glue has dried enough to handle the pendant, remove any pins and turn the pendant over. Use the

tip of a pin or a paper-piecing tool to apply a small dot of glue on the back of each join as reinforcement. Allow the glue to dry.

7 Brush a thin coating of fixative on the back surface, if desired. Be sure to clear fixative from the hole in the top domed tight coil. Allow the pendant to dry completely, preferably overnight.

8 Use 2 pairs of jewelry pliers to twist open a jump ring. Slip it through the top domed tight coil and close it by reversing the twisting motion **(Figure 7)**. Slip a necklace chain through the jump ring.

tip : *Use a straight pin to clear glue from the center hole of one of the domed tight coils to allow for the insertion of a jump ring in step 8.*

5 Referring to **Figure 6**, assemble the coils on a nonstick work board as shown or create your own abstract design. Place the domed tight coil with a glue-free center hole at the top of the pendant.

FINISHED SIZE
The diameter of each
earring is ¾" (2 cm).

SHAPES USED
Tight coil

MATERIALS
Ivory with silver edge
quilling paper

Black with copper edge
quilling paper

2 silver-tone 6 mm
jump rings

2 silver-tone 4 mm
jump rings

2 silver-tone ear wires

TOOLS
Quilling tool

Glue

Small scissors

Ruler

Fine-tip tweezers

Ball-head pin

Paper-piercing tool

Nonstick work board

Plastic lid or fine-tip
glue bottle

Damp cloth or
paper towel

2 pairs of flat-nose or
chain-nose jewelry pliers

Fixative

Watercolor brush

Sculptured Disc EARRINGS

Pretty copper- and silver-edge papers are
used to make these mixed-metal sculptured
discs. The dangle earrings have a brilliant
shine, while the black and ivory paper strips
give an interesting striped effect to the
reverse side of the earrings.

Working with Varied-Width Strips:

Occasionally quilling strips from different packages have not been factory-cut to exactly the same width. In this case, align them as best you can so the gilded edges match up evenly and the earring discs will have a perfectly smooth surface.

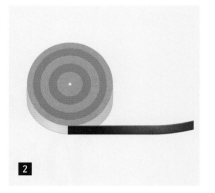

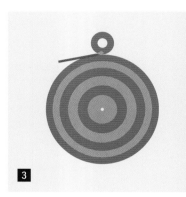

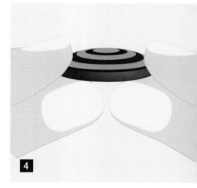

FOR EACH EARRING:

1 Roll a 7" (18 cm) ivory with silver edge paper strip on a slotted tool. Glue the bluntly cut end. Put a small amount of glue on one end of a 9" (23 cm) black with copper edge strip with bluntly cut ends and butt it against the end of the first strip **(Figure 1)**. Roll the black with copper edge strip and glue the end.

note: *You may find it easier to slip the disc off the tool before adding the next strip in step 2.*

2 In the same manner, roll the following full-length (17" [43 cm]) strips around the coil by hand one at a time in this order: 1 silver, 1 copper, 1 silver, and 1 copper **(Figure 2)**.

tip: *Use just your finger pads, not your nails, when wrapping strips by hand and shaping discs to avoid scratching the metallic finish.*

3 Roll a 3½" (9 cm) black with copper edge strip on the tip of a paper-piercing tool or a cocktail stick (round toothpick) to create a tight coil with a center hole large enough to accommodate a jump ring. Glue the end in place. Glue this tight coil to one edge ("the top") of the earring disc so that the 2 ends meet and are hidden **(Figure 3)**.

4 Press the metallic surface of the earring disc gently with your fingertip pads to create a smooth, concave surface **(Figure 4)**.

5

A light coating of fixative on the back of the Sculptured Disc Earrings helps preserve the curve.

5 Brush a thin coating of fixative on the earring back to preserve the curve.

6 Apply a dot of glue where the two coils join as additional reinforcement.

7 When the back of the earring is dry, brush a thin coating of glue on the front to protect the solid surface. (Unlike matte fixative, clear glue will not diminish the metallic shine.)

8 When the fixative and glue have dried completely, open the 6 mm jump ring and slip it through the hole in the tight coil. Close the jump ring. Slip on an open 4 mm jump ring. Slip an ear wire onto the jump ring and close the jump ring **(Figure 5)**.

FINISHED SIZE
Pendant measures
1¼" × 2¾" (3.2 cm
× 7 cm).

SHAPES USED
Hand-sculpted outline

Marquise ring coil

MATERIALS
Black with gold edge
quilling paper

Gold-tone 9 mm
jump ring

Gold-tone necklace
chain of choice

TOOLS
Quilling tool

Glue

Small scissors

Ruler

Fine-tip tweezers

Ball-head pins

Paper-piercing tool

¼" (6 mm) dowel

⅛" (3 mm) dowel

Nonstick work board

Plastic lid or fine-tip
glue bottle

Damp cloth or
paper towel

2 pairs of flat-nose or
chain-nose jewelry pliers

Fixative (optional)

Watercolor brush
(optional)

Solitary Leaf PENDANT

Wow everyone you meet when wearing this abstract leaf pendant. Each time I make it, the outline looks a bit different than the time before. No worries, it always resembles a natural leaf. They come in many sizes and shapes, after all.

note: When working with a double- or triple-thick strip, one that has been made by gluing strips one on top of another, let the glue dry completely, then run the strip between your fingers or over a tool handle as if you were curling ribbon. This will help soften the strip so it can be easily shaped.

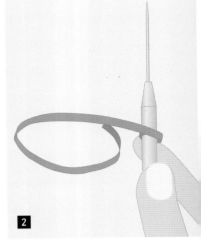

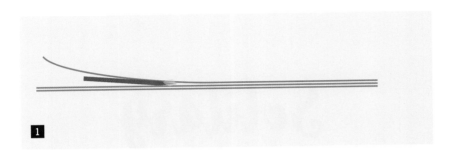

1 Glue three 12" (30.5 cm) strips together, one on top of another with the metallic edges facing the same direction (**Figure 1**). (For tips, see Creating Thicker Strips in Chapter 2.) When the glue is completely dry, trim the strip to 9" (23 cm).

2 Wrap one end of the strip firmly around a ¼" (6 mm) dowel for the first revolution to create a curled loop, then with relaxed finger pressure continue rolling the strip loosely to the end to give it a training curve (**Figure 2**).

3 Slip the strip off the dowel and glue the curled end to the strip (**Figure 3**).

4 Continue shaping the strip with your fingers. Pinch and curve the tail of the strip about 2¾" (7 cm) from the end. Glue the 2 layers together at the pinched fold to create the leaf tip (**Figure 4**). Hold the tip while the glue sets, about a minute or two (**Figure 5**).

5 Curve the remainder of the strip to meet the initial curl, creating the top curve of the leaf outline. Trim the excess strip length, then glue the end and the curl in place, holding them until the glue sets (**Figure 6**).

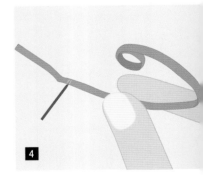

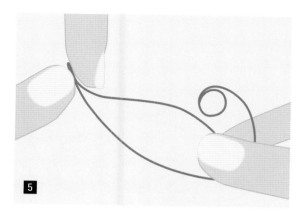

5

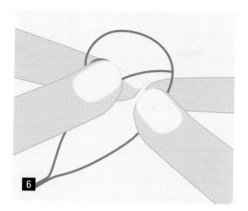

6

6 Referring to **Figure 7**, cut the remaining piece of the triple-layer strip so it is the exact length of the interior of the leaf (this will be the center vein). Glue one end at each side of the leaf-shape interior.

7 Roll a 3¼" (8.5 cm) single strip around a ¼" (6 mm) dowel. Slip the coil off the tool and pinch it at opposite points to create a marquise ring coil with a width of about ⅜" (1 cm) **(Figure 8)**. Glue the end at the point and trim the excess paper. Make 10 total.

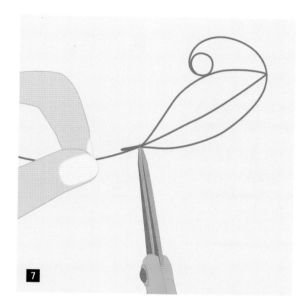

7

8

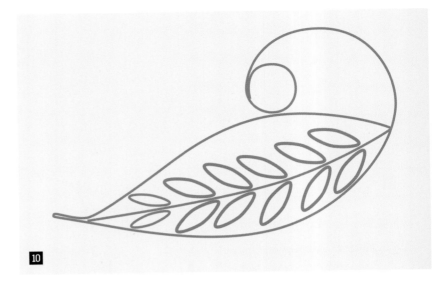

9

8 Roll a 2¾" (7 cm) single strip around a dowel that is a bit larger than ⅛" (3 mm). Slip the coil off the dowel and pinch it at opposite points to create a marquise ring coil with a width of about ¼" (6 mm) (**Figure 9**). Glue the end and trim the excess paper. Make 2 total. (As an alternative to rolling such small ring coils, you may prefer the folding method outlined in Marquise Coils for the Masses.)

9 Position and glue these marquise ring coils evenly along each side of the center vein. The 2 smallest coils will be positioned opposite one another at the leaf tip (**Figure 10**).

10 When the glue has dried enough to handle the leaf, turn it over and apply a small dot of glue with the tip of a pin or paper-piercing tool on each join as reinforcement. Brush a light coating of fixative on the back of the leaf when the glue dots have dried, if desired. Allow the leaf to dry completely, preferably overnight.

11 Use 2 pairs of jewelry pliers to twist open a jump ring and slip it through the curl. Reverse the twisting motion to close the jump ring. Slide a necklace chain through the jump ring.

10

Marquise Coils for the Masses

Instead of rolling such small ring coils, you might find it easier to fold them. Make a fold at the end of a strip that measures the width of the desired ring coil. Continue folding the strip 4 times around the initial fold. Glue the end and trim the excess paper. Also glue the interior (starting) end in place. Hold the ends (points) between your thumb and index finger, and gently pinch to curve the sides.

For extra durability, apply dots of glue on the back of the pendant along the center vein by each marquise ring coil and where the curl meets the leaf.

FINISHED SIZE
Pendant measures
1⅛" × 2⅛" (2.8 cm
× 5.3 cm).

SHAPES USED
Marquise ring coil

Domed tight coil

Tight coil

MATERIALS
Black with gold edge
quilling paper

2 gold-tone 4 mm
jump rings

24" (61 cm) gold-tone
chain of choice

TOOLS
Quilling tool

Glue

Small scissors

Ruler

Fine-tip tweezers

Ball-head pins

Paper-piercing tool

⅜" (1 cm) dowel

¼" (6 mm) dowel

Nonstick work board

Plastic lid or fine-tip
glue bottle

Damp cloth or
paper towel

2 pairs of flat-nose or
chain-nose jewelry pliers

Fixative (optional)

Watercolor brush
(optional)

Deconstructed Flower PENDANT

Not only is this design a fairly easy one to
quill and assemble, but it is striking in its
simplicity.

1 Roll a 6½" (16.5 cm) strip around a ⅜" (1 cm) dowel. Slip the coil off the dowel and pinch it at opposite points to create a marquise ring coil with a width of about ½" (1.3 cm). Glue the end and trim the excess paper. Put a dot of glue on the interior strip end to hold it in place **(Figure 1)**. Make 14 total.

2 Roll a 4¼" (11 cm) strip around a ¼" (6 mm) dowel. Slip the coil off the dowel and pinch it at opposite points to create a marquise ring coil with a width of about ⅜" (1 cm). Glue the end and trim the excess paper. Put a dot of glue on the interior strip end to hold it in place. Make 2 total.

3 Roll a 4" (10 cm) strip on a quilling tool to make a domed tight coil for the flower center. Apply glue with the tip of a pin or paper-piecing tool inside the coil to preserve the curved shape **(Figure 2)**.

4 Roll a 2" (5 cm) strip on the tip of a paper-piercing tool or a round toothpick to create a tight coil with a center hole large enough to accommodate a jump ring **(Figure 3)**. Make 2 total.

5 Arrange the quilled components on a nonstick work board **(Figure 4)**, using pins if desired. Note that the jump-ring coils are positioned black side up to add a bit of interest. Glue the components together.

6 When the glue has dried enough to handle the pendant, turn it over and apply a small dot of glue with the tip of a pin or paper-piercing tool on each join as reinforcement **(Figure 5)**. When the glue is dry, brush a thin coating of fixative on the pendant back for additional durability, if desired.

7 Allow the pendant to dry completely, preferably overnight. Using 2 pairs of jewelry pliers, twist open the jump rings and insert one into each ring coil. Then insert one end of a 24" (61 cm) chain (long enough to slip over your head) into each jump ring. Reverse the twisting motion to close the jump rings.

Glue Be Gone

Use a damp cloth to gently wipe away any stray glue marks on outer-most coil edges while they are still wet. Excess glue leaves a telltale shine, especially on black quilling paper.

FINISHED SIZE
Pendant measures
1⅛" × 2" (2.8 cm × 5 cm).

SHAPES USED
Marquise ring coil

Marquise coil

MATERIALS
Black with gold edge
quilling paper

Pearlized gold quilling
paper

Gold-tone 6 mm
jump ring

Gold-tone necklace
chain of choice

TOOLS
Quilling tool

Glue

Small scissors

Ruler

Fine-tip tweezers

Ball-head pins

Paper-piercing tool

1½" (3.8 cm) dowel

Nonstick work board

Plastic lid or fine-tip
glue bottle

Damp cloth or
paper towel

2 pairs of flat-nose or
chain-nose jewelry pliers

Fixative (optional)

Watercolor brush
(optional)

Leafy Vine
PENDANT

———

This elegant design makes me think of a trellis-climbing vine. Nearly all of the marquises are the same size, which makes it a rather quick project. I outlined the outermost edge of the oval marquise with one layer of a pearlized gold strip to nicely finish the frame.

1 Make the marquise ring coil frame: Join together a full-length (17" [43 cm]) black with gold edge strip and a 2" (5 cm) black with gold edge strip by slightly overlapping the torn ends and gluing them together. **(Figure 1)**.

2 Roll this 19" (48.5 cm) strip around a 1½" (3.8 cm) dowel to create a ring coil. Slide it off the dowel and pinch at opposite points to create a marquise shape **(Figure 2)**. Put a dot of glue on the interior strip end to hold it in place.

tip : *If there are gaps between the coil layers, fill them with small dots of glue placed on the tip of a pin, working from the reverse side so as to not mar the metallic surface.*

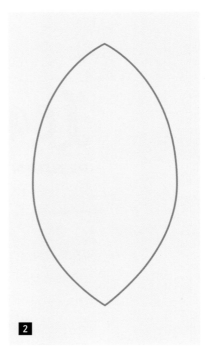

3 Apply a thin coating of glue to the outer edge of the frame with a pin, paper-piercing tool, or your fingertip **(Figure 3)**. Adhere one pearlized gold strip layer as an outline, lining up the ends closely together at one pointed end **(Figure 4)**. This will be the top of the pendant because the jump ring will hide the join.

4 To make the leaf stems, create a double-thickness strip by gluing two 6" (15 cm) strips, one on top of the other, with the metallic edges facing the same direction. Let the glue dry, then gently curve the strip by running it between your fingers **(Figure 5)**. Cut the strip into 5 smaller pieces, replicating the vines in the pendant photo to fit the frame. Glue one end of each stem in place within the frame **(Figure 6)**.

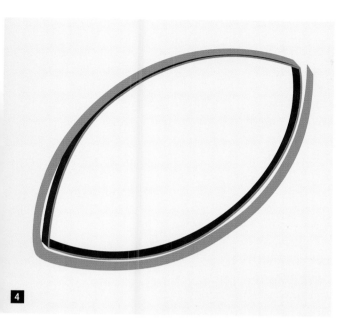

4

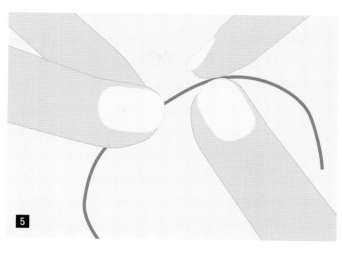

5

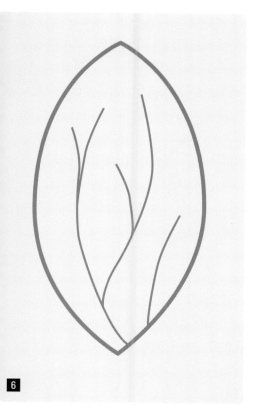

6

5 Make 20 marquise coils for the leaves using 2½" (6.5 cm) strips.

6 Arrange the marquise coil leaves in pairs and singles along the stems, reserving any marquise coils that happened to be rolled slightly smaller than the others for placement at the stem tips **(Figure 7)**. Glue in place. Also glue the leaf tips that are nearest the frame to the frame interior **(Figure 8)**.

7 When the glue has dried enough to handle the pendant, turn it over and apply a small dot of glue on each join with the tip of a pin or paper-piercing tool as reinforcement. When the dots of glue have dried, brush a thin coating of fixative onto the pendant back for additional durability, if desired.

8 Allow the pendant to dry completely, preferably overnight. Using 2 pairs of jewelry pliers, twist open a jump ring. Slip it through the top point of the frame and reverse the twisting motion to close it. Slide a necklace chain through the ring.

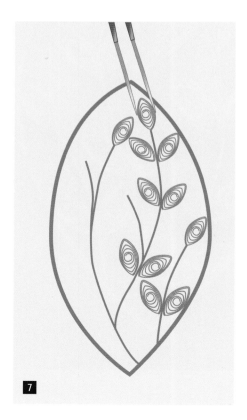

7

8

The graceful lines of the Leafy Vine Pendant are reinforced with extra dots of glue on the back of the design.

FINISHED SIZE
Pendant measures
1⅛" × 2" (2.8 cm × 5 cm).

SHAPES USED
Marquise coil

MATERIALS
Ivory with gold edge
quilling paper

Pearlized gold quilling
paper (for the bail)

Gold-tone necklace
chain of choice

TOOLS
Quilling tool

Glue

Small scissors

Ruler

Fine-tip tweezers

Ball-head pins

Paper-piercing tool

Nonstick work board

Plastic lid or fine-tip
glue bottle

Damp cloth or
paper towel

Fixative (optional)

Watercolor brush
(optional)

A Girl's Best Friend

PENDANT

This is one of my very favorite designs
because I admire geometric shapes,
especially the dramatic diamond. Brand-new
quillers will enjoy making this gilded pendant
because it features just one type of coil, the
marquise.

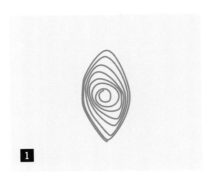

1 Make 17 marquise coils using 3½" (9 cm) strips of ivory with gold edge quilling paper **(Figure 1)**.

2 Use tweezers to arrange and glue the marquise coils snugly together to form a diamond shape **(Figure 2)**. Place 1 marquise horizontally at the top.

3 Make a metallic-paper bail: Trim the width of a ⅛" × 3" (3 mm × 7.5 cm) strip of pearlized gold quilling paper so it is slightly narrower than ⅛" (3 mm) **(Figure 3)**. (This gives a finer look in proportion to the scale of the pendant.) Fold down one end of the strip about ¼" (6 mm), then wrap the strip around the initial fold 4 times **(Figure 4)**. Glue the end and trim the excess paper. Apply a tiny amount of glue to the strip end inside the coil to hold it in place.

4 Center the paper bail vertically on the horizontal marquise and glue it in place **(Figure 5)**.

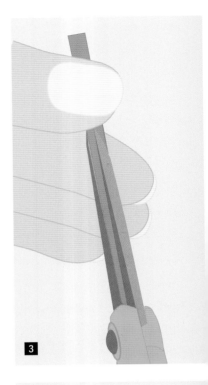

5 When the glue has dried enough to handle the pendant, turn it over and apply a small dot of glue with the tip of a pin or a paper-piercing tool on each join as reinforcement. When the glue has dried, brush a light coating of fixative onto the back of the pendant, if desired.

6 Let the glue and fixative dry completely, preferably overnight. Then slide a necklace chain through the paper bail.

This reverse view of A Girl's Best Friend Pendant showcases the subtle shine of the simple, yet striking pearlized paper bail.

FINISHED SIZE
Pendant measures
1⅝" × 2⅜" (4 × 6 cm).

SHAPES USED
Loose scroll

S scroll

Shaped marquise

MATERIALS
Black with gold edge
quilling paper

Gold-tone 9 mm
jump ring

Gold-tone necklace
chain of choice

TOOLS
Quilling tool

Glue

Small scissors

Ruler

Fine-tip tweezers

Ball-head pins

Paper-piercing tool

¼" (6 mm) dowel

Nonstick work board

Plastic lid or fine-tip
glue bottle

Damp cloth or
paper towel

2 pairs of flat-nose or
chain-nose jewelry pliers

Fixative (optional)

Watercolor brush
(optional)

Loops & Leaves

PENDANT

—

The first time I wore this pendant I was at an art exhibit. A woman walked past, then stopped suddenly and backed up to peer closely at it. She apologized for her curiosity, but of course I didn't mind. I was delighted that my quilled necklace had caught her attention amid so many beautiful paintings. When I told her I had made it, she asked where I had learned to work with metal. She looked at me incredulously when I said the pendant was made of rolled paper. Turning the world onto paper jewelry one person at a time!

1 Make 10 shaped marquise coils using 4" (10 cm) strips.

2 Apply a thin coating of glue to one long edge of a shaped marquise coil as shown **(Figure 1)**. Press a second shaped marquise coil against the glue to create a leaf pair **(Figure 2)**. Pinch and hold the 2 shapes together until the glue sets, about a minute or two. Repeat with the remaining coils to make 5 leaf-pair sets.

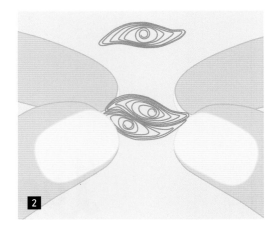

3 Stack and glue three 15" (38 cm) strips, one on top of another, with the metallic edges facing the same direction to create a triple-strength strip. Let the glue dry *completely* (otherwise, the strips will separate and buckle when rolled).

4 Cut the 15" (38 cm) strip into one 4½" (11.5 cm) strip and three 3½" (9 cm) strips. Make an S scroll with the 4½" (11.5 cm) strip and 3 loose scrolls with the 3½" (9 cm) strips by rolling the end of each strip firmly around a ¼" (6 mm) dowel **(Figure 3)**.

note: *For tips on curling layered strips, see Handling Thicker Strips in Chapter 2.*

5 Referring to **Figure 4**, glue 2 loose scrolls to the S scroll as shown, then glue on the remaining loose scroll. Next, glue the leaves in place **(Figure 5)**.

6 When the glue has dried enough to handle the pendant, turn it over and apply a small dot of glue with the tip of a pin or paper-piercing tool on each join as reinforcement. Let the glue dry, then brush a light coating of fixative onto the back of the pendant, if desired. Let the glue and fixative dry completely, preferably overnight.

7 Using 2 pairs of jewelry pliers, twist open a jump ring and insert it through the top loop of the S scroll. Reverse the twisting motion to close the jump ring and slide a necklace chain through it.

FINISHED SIZE
Lotus blossom measures
1⅝" × 2⅝" (4 × 6.5 cm).

Disc measures ⅞" × 1"
(2.2 × 2.5 cm).

SHAPES USED
Marquise ring coil

Triangle ring coil

Domed tight coil

Tight coil

MATERIALS
Ivory with gold edge
quilling paper

Ivory with silver edge
quilling paper

Pearlized gold quilling
paper

2 brass-tone 6 mm
jump rings

24" (61 cm) brass-
tone chain

TOOLS
Quilling tool

Glue

Small scissors

Ruler

Fine-tip tweezers

Ball-head pins

Paper-piercing tool

⅞" (2.2 cm) dowel

⅜" (1 cm) dowel

Nonstick work board

Plastic lid or fine-tip
glue bottle

Damp cloth or
paper towel

Metallic gold acrylic paint

Watercolor brush

2 pairs of flat-nose or
chain-nose jewelry pliers

Fixative (optional)

Petal Power

LARIAT NECKLACE

This stylish necklace makes me think of
a lotus flower in bloom. Not only is it a
guaranteed attention-getter, but it is also
easy on/easy off because the chain is long
enough to slip over your head. But if you
would rather not threaten your hairstyle, you
can simply slip the domed tight coil in and
out through the far right petal.

MAKING THE LOTUS FLOWER:

1 Roll a full-length (17" [43 cm]) ivory with gold edge strip around a ⅞" (2.2 cm) dowel. Slip the ring coil off the dowel, then pinch it where the strip started and at the opposite point to create a marquise ring coil **(Figure 1)**. Glue the end as shown **(Figure 2)** and trim the excess paper. Glue the starting end of the strip in place inside the marquise ring coil **(Figure 3)**.

2 Glue a pearlized gold strip around the outside of the marquise ring coil as shown **(Figure 4)**. Glue the end and trim the excess paper **(Figure 5)**. Make 5 lotus petals total.

3 Roll a 6" (15 cm) ivory with gold edge strip around a ⅜" (1 cm) dowel **(Figure 6)**. Slide the strip off the dowel and pinch it close to the interior strip end to make a teardrop ring coil. Pinch the coil 2 more times to make a triangular shape **(Figure 7)**. Glue the end and trim the excess paper. Outline this triangular ring coil with a pearlized gold strip by gluing it once around the perimeter. Glue the end and trim the excess paper. Make a total of 3 triangular ring coil petals in varied shapes **(Figure 8)**.

4 Referring to **Figure 9**, assemble the 2-layer lotus blossom on a nonstick work board. Glue 2 petals together at their bases, then glue the 3 triangles to the base of this petal pair to make the bottom layer. Glue the remaining 3 petals together at their bases for the top layer. Glue the 2 layers together so that the 3-petal layer is centered on top of the 2-petal layer.

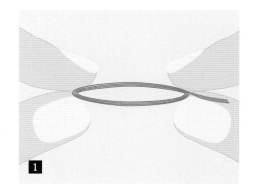

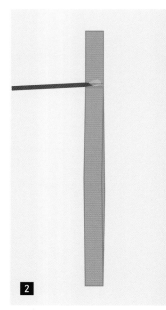

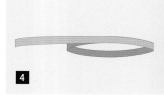

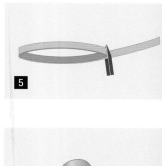

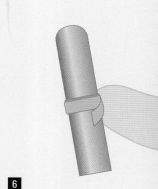

7

8

9

When the glue has dried enough to handle the lotus, turn it over and apply a small dot of glue with the tip of a pin or paper-piercing tool on each join s reinforcement. Allow the glue to dry, then brush a thin coating of fixative on the back of the lotus for additional durability, if desired.

Use 2 pairs of jewelry pliers to twist open a jump ring and slip it onto the top point of the bottom layer of the far-left petal, then slide one end of the chain onto the jump ring. Reverse the twisting motion to close the jump ring. Set aside.

Gluing the Strips

When outlining the lotus petals, striped disc, and connecting ring coil with pearlized gold quilling paper, you will only need to glue at the beginning and end, not the entire strip length. If you do get glue on the outer edge, gently wipe it off the strip with a damp cloth or paper towel while it is still wet. Because pearlized quilling paper has a light plastic coating, wiping it will not affect the metallic shine. Even regular quilling paper can withstand a gentle damp wiping to remove freshly applied glue, if necessary.

MAKING THE PENDANT DISC:

note: *The ⅞" (2.2 cm) diameter striped disc attaches to the necklace chain with a jump ring and slides through the far-right lotus petal, dangling loosely 2–3" (5–7.5 cm) below the flower.*

7 Roll a 7" (18 cm) strip of ivory with gold-edge paper with bluntly cut ends on a slotted tool and glue the end in place. Put a small amount of glue on one end of a full-length (17" [43 cm]) strip of ivory with silver-edge paper and butt the end against the end of the first strip. Roll the strip completely and glue the end **(Figure 10)**.

tip: *You may find it easiest to slip the disc off the tool at this point and continue rolling by hand.*

Continue rolling in the same manner, adding 2 full strips of ivory with gold-edge paper, 2 full strips of ivory with silver edge paper, and 1 full strip of ivory with gold edge paper. Outline the coil by gluing a pearlized gold strip once around the perimeter. Trim the excess paper and glue the end **(Figure 11)**.

note: *Avoid pressing on the metallic surface of the gilded strips with sharp fingernails or tools because they will mar the shiny surface.*

8 Roll a 3½" (9 cm) ivory with gold-edge strip on the tip of a paper-piercing tool or a round toothpick to create a tight coil with a center hole large enough to accommodate a jump ring. Glue the end in place. Outline the coil by gluing a pearlized gold strip once around the perimeter. Trim the excess paper and glue the end **(Figure 12)**.

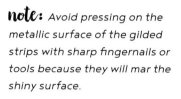

9 Glue this small coil to the striped tight coil where the seams meet so they are hidden **(Figure 13)**. Let the glue dry.

10 Dome the striped tight coil by gently pressing on the underside with your fingertip pads. Brush a layer of metallic gold paint on the inside curve of the dome to preserve the shape.

note: *Because the striped disc will swing freely and may flip over when worn, the metallic paint not only preserves the curve, it also provides a finished look.*

11 When the paint is dry, apply a small amount of glue to the join as reinforcement. When the glue is dry, brush on a thin coating of fixative, if desired.

12 Brush a thin layer of clear glue on the front of the dome to protect it.

note: *Unlike a matte fixative, which can dull the shine of metallic-edge strips, glue dries clear and glossy. Let the glue dry completely, preferably overnight.*

13 Use 2 pairs of jewelry pliers to twist open a jump ring and insert it into the tight coil center, then slide the free end of the necklace chain onto the same jump ring. Reverse the twisting motion to close the jump ring.

The striped disc slides through the top layer, far-right petal.

FINISHED SIZE
Pendant measures 2⅛"
(5.3 cm) square.

SHAPES USED
Square ring coil

Single scroll

Double scroll

MATERIALS
Ivory with gold edge
quilling paper

Ivory with silver edge
quilling paper

Pearlized gold
quilling paper

Gold-tone or silver-tone
7 mm jump ring

Gold-tone or silver-tone
necklace chain of choice

TOOLS
Quilling tool

Glue

Small scissors

Ruler

Fine-tip tweezers

Ball-head pins

Paper-piercing tool

1¾" (4.5 cm) dowel or
1¾" (4.5 cm) square box

Nonstick work board

Plastic lid or fine-tip
glue bottle

Damp cloth or
paper towel

2 pairs of flat-nose or
chain-nose jewelry pliers

Fixative (optional)

Watercolor brush
(optional)

Swirled Scrolls PENDANT

Make a statement with this contemporary
tilted square filled with swirling scrolls. As a
bonus, you'll become a scroll-rolling expert!

note: *Use a needle tool or regular slotted tool instead of a superfine slotted tool for this project. Double scrolls require 2 strips to be rolled at once, and 2 strips will not fit into the superfine slot.*

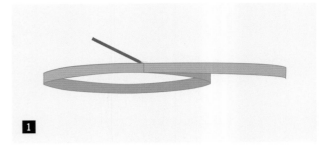

1 Make the pendant frame: Create a 4-layer ring coil by rolling a full-length 17" (43 cm) ivory with silver edge strip with bluntly cut ends around a 1¾" (4.5 cm) dowel. Glue the end. Butt and glue a 6½" (16.5 cm) strip of the same type of paper against the end of the first strip, roll, and glue the end **(Figure 1)**. Slip the coil off the dowel.

tip: Roll the strips firmly but loosely enough so that the completed ring coil can be slid off the dowel.

2 When the glue is dry, pinch a point close to the interior strip end and at the opposite side to create the marquise ring coil. Turn the coil 90 degrees and pinch 2 more opposite points **(Figure 2)**. Put a dot of glue on the interior strip end to hold it in place.

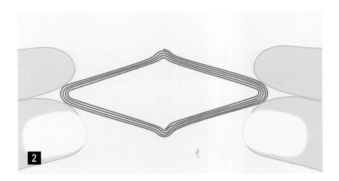

Using a Square Form

An alternative method to make a pendant frame is to use a square form (a small box) instead of a dowel. For this project, you would use a 1¾" (4.5 cm) box. Wrap an ivory with silver edge strip around the circumference 4 times, applying a small amount of glue at each corner turn. When the strip is close to the end, glue it at a corner, and trim the excess paper. Attach another strip, aligning it against the previous strip end, and continue wrapping from the same corner.

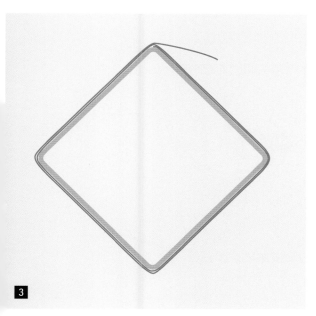

3

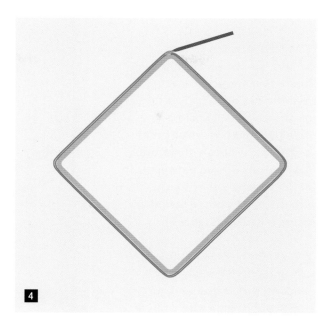

4

5

3 Outline the square ring coil by gluing a pearlized gold strip around the perimeter twice (**Figure 3**). Finish by gluing the strip at a corner and cutting the excess paper. Fill any gaps between the frame layers with tiny dots of glue placed on the tip of a pin. Work from the back of the frame so as not to mar the metallic surface (**Figure 4**).

4 Make a variety of scrolls in different sizes using a mix of silver-edge and gold-edge strips (**Figure 5**). As a guideline, the largest double scrolls require two 4" (10 cm) strips each, and the single scrolls use strips of varied lengths from 2" to 3" (5 to 7½ cm).

5 Starting at the corners, arrange the scrolls in the square frame to achieve a balanced design. Glue just the tail of each scroll to hold it in place **(Figure 6)**. When all of the scroll tails have been glued, apply tiny amounts of glue between the scrolls where they touch with the tip of a pin to hold them securely in place **(Figure 7)**.

6 When the glue has dried enough to handle the pendant, turn it over and apply a small dot of glue with a pin or paper-piercing tool on each join as reinforcement. A light coating of fixative may be brushed onto the back of the pendant, if desired, taking care to not overly saturate the scrolls as this would cause them to swell.

7 Use 2 pairs of jewelry pliers to twist open a jump ring and slip it onto one corner of the square; the necklace will hang from that point as a diamond shape. Reverse the twisting motion to close the jump ring and slide a necklace chain through it.

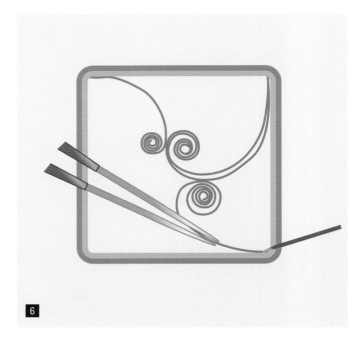

6

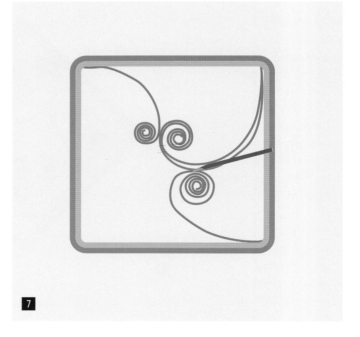

7

A tiny dot of glue applied where each scroll meets adds to their delicate strength.

FINISHED SIZE
Pendant measures
1⅜" × 1¾" (3.5 × 4.5 cm).

SHAPES USED
Modified rectangle
ring coil

Double scroll

Domed tight coil

Teardrop coil

Shaped teardrop coil

MATERIALS
Ivory with gold edge
quilling paper

Pearlized gold quilling
paper (for the bail)

Gold-tone necklace
chain of choice

TOOLS
Quilling tool

Glue

Small scissors

Ruler

Fine-tip tweezers

Ball-head pins

Paper-piercing tool

1¼" (3.2 cm) dowel

Nonstick work board

Plastic lid or fine-tip
glue bottle

Damp cloth or
paper towel

Fixative (optional)

Watercolor brush
(optional)

Classic Filigree
PENDANT

I created this pendant, which combines a variety of elegant scrolls and coils, soon after my first package of gilded paper arrived in the mail. So impressed by the smooth metallic shine, I knew immediately that a new world–a jewelry-making world–was at my fingertips. Enjoy the compliments you'll receive whenever you wear this small beauty.

Make Coils Match: *Pay special attention to the placement of the inner coil rotations of the ivory with gold edge teardrops and shaped teardrops so that your shapes resemble the ones in the example. When making coil pairs with metallic-edge paper, such as the teardrop heart pair, shaped teardrops, and double scrolls, roll one of the coils with the metallic edge facing up on your tool and the other coil with the metallic edge facing down. When the 2 teardrop coils are placed together to make a heart, for example, the metallic edge will show on both sides of the heart front, and their inner coil rotations will meet.*

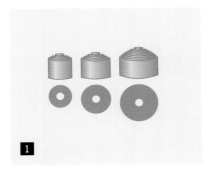

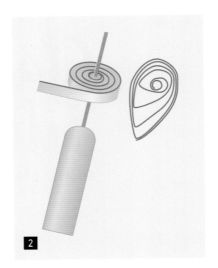

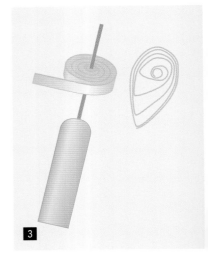

1 Make 7 domed tight coils using one 1½" (3.8 cm) strip, three 2" (5 cm) strips, and three 2½" (6.4 cm) strips **(Figure 1)**. Set the domed tight coils aside.

2 Make 4 teardrop coils using 5" (12.5 cm) strips. Roll 2 of the strips with the metallic edge facing up **(Figure 2)** and 2 with the metallic edge facing down **(Figure 3)**. Set aside.

3 In the same manner as step 2, make 4 shaped teardrop coils using 4" (10 cm) strips and 2 double scrolls with two 2" (5 cm) strips. Roll half of the strips in each group with the metallic edge facing up and half with the metallic edge facing down **(Figure 4)**.

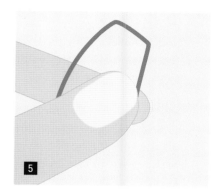

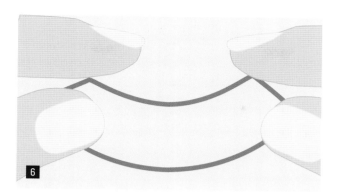

4 Roll a full-length (17" [43 cm]) strip around a 1¼" (3.2 cm) dowel to make a 4-layer ring coil. Create a modified rectangular ring coil with curved upper and lower lines by pinching a point close to the interior strip end and at the opposite side to create a marquise ring coil, then rotating the coil ⅜" (1 cm) and pinching 2 opposite points **(Figures 5 and 6)**.

5 Glue the 2 double scrolls and three 2½" (6.5 cm) domed tight coils inside the modified rectangular ring coil as shown **(Figure 7)**.

6 Glue two 5" (12.5 cm) teardrop coils together to form a heart shape. Glue a 1½" (3.8 cm) domed tight coil to the point of the heart, then glue a 5" (12.5 cm) teardrop on each side of the domed tight coil **(Figure 8)**.

7 Glue three 2" (5 cm) domed tight coils and four 4" (10 cm) shaped teardrops around the heart **(Figure 9)**.

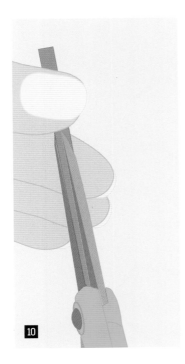

10

11

8 Glue the heart-shaped section to the top of the base.

9 Make a metallic-paper bail: Trim the width of a ⅛" × 3" (3 mm × 7.5 cm) strip of pearlized gold quilling paper so that it is slightly narrower than ⅛" (3 mm) **(Figure 10)**. (This gives a finer look in proportion to the scale of the pendant.) Fold down one end of the strip about ¼" (6 mm) and wrap the strip around the initial fold 4 times **(Figure 11)**. Glue the end and trim the excess paper. Apply a tiny amount of glue to the strip end inside the coil to hold it in place. Glue it between the top pair of shaped teardrops as shown **(Figure 12)**.

10 Turn the pendant over and apply a small dot of glue with the tip of a pin or paper-piercing tool on each join as reinforcement. Brush a light coating of fixative onto the back of the pendant, if desired, taking care to not overly saturate the coils and scrolls as this would cause them to swell.

11 Let the glue and fixative dry completely, preferably overnight, then slide a necklace chain through the paper bail.

12

The narrow
paper bail fits
perfectly between
the Shaped
Teardrop Coils
for a professional
looking finish.

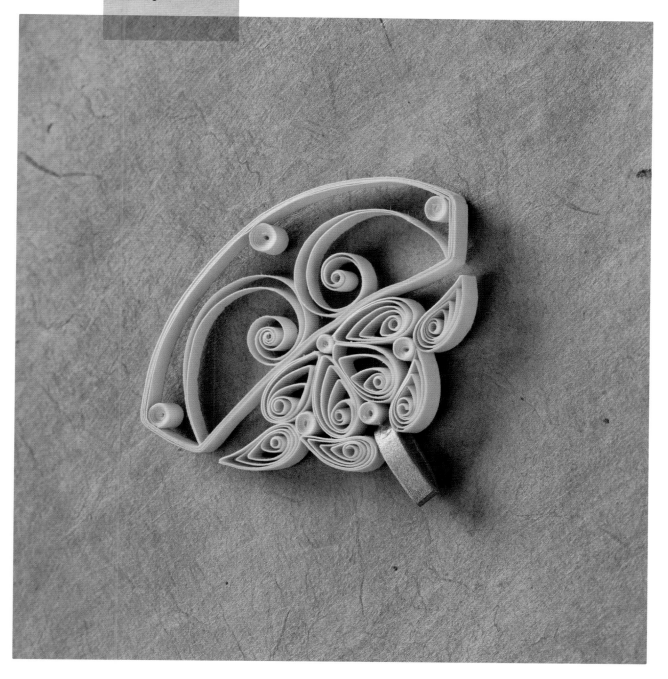

FINISHED SIZE
Each earring measures
⅝" × ⅞" (1.5 × 2.2 cm).

SHAPES USED
Teardrop ring coil

Loose scroll

MATERIALS
Black with gold edge
quilling paper

Pearlized gold quilling
paper

2 gold-tone 5 mm
jump rings

2 gold-tone 4 mm
jump rings

2 gold-tone earring
wires

TOOLS
Quilling tool

Glue

Small scissors

Ruler

Fine-tip tweezers

Ball-head pins

Paper-piercing tool

¾" (2 cm) dowel

⅜" (1 cm) dowel

Nonstick work board

Plastic lid or fine-tip
glue bottle

Damp cloth or
paper towel

2 pairs of flat-nose or
chain-nose jewelry pliers

Fixative (optional)

Watercolor brush
(optional)

Teardrop Scroll EARRINGS

This intricate pair of teardrop-within-a-teardrop earrings will swing gently as you move and catch the light due to their golden shine.

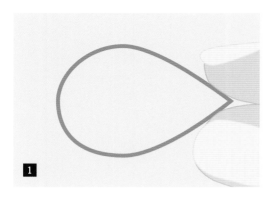

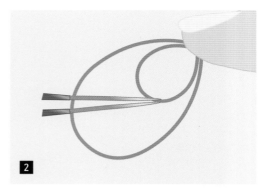

FOR EACH EARRING:

1 Roll an 11" (28 cm) strip of black with gold edge quilling paper around a ¾" (2 cm) dowel. Slide the ring coil off the dowel and pinch it close to the interior cut end to create a teardrop ring coil (**Figure 1**). Glue the end and trim the excess paper. Then glue the loose end in place inside the teardrop ring coil.

2 In the same manner as step 1, make the smaller teardrop ring coil by rolling a 5" (12.5 cm) strip of black with gold edge quilling paper around a ⅜" (1 cm) dowel. Glue one layer of pearlized gold quilling paper around the perimeter of the coil. Glue the pointed end of this teardrop ring coil inside the larger ring coil so that the points meet (**Figure 2**).

3 Make 7 loose scrolls using 3" (7.5 cm) strips of black with gold edge quilling paper. Arrange the scrolls inside the large teardrop ring coil as shown, trimming the tails as needed so the scrolls evenly fill the space (**Figure 3**). Adhere the tails to the

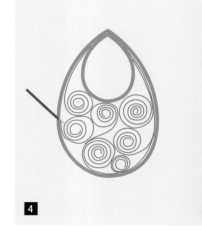

inside of the ring coil and to one another where they meet, using tiny amounts of glue applied with the tip of a pin (**Figure 4**).

4 When the glue is dry, turn the earrings over and apply a small dot of glue with the tip of a pin or paper-piercing tool on each join as reinforcement. Brush a light coating of fixative on the reverse side, if desired, taking care to not overly saturate the scrolls as this would cause them to swell. Let the glue and fixative dry completely, preferably overnight.

5 Use 2 pairs of jewelry pliers to twist open a 5 mm jump ring and slip it through the teardrop ring-coil point. Reverse the twisting motion to close the jump ring. Slip an open 4 mm jump ring onto the first jump ring. Slip an ear wire onto the jump ring. Close the jump ring.

The reverse side of the Teardrop Scroll Earrings showing dots of glue at joins as reinforcement.

Golden Wreath PENDANT

FINISHED SIZE
Pendant measures 1¾"
× 2¼" (4.5 × 5.5 cm).

SHAPES USED
S scroll

Domed tight coil

MATERIALS
Ivory with gold edge
quilling paper

Pearlized gold quilling
paper (for the bail)

Gold-tone necklace
chain of choice

TOOLS
Quilling tool

Glue

Small scissors

Ruler

Fine-tip tweezers

Paper-piercing tool

Ball-head pins

Nonstick work board

Plastic lid or fine-tip
glue bottle

Damp cloth or
paper towel

Fixative

Watercolor brush

While this pendant has a delicate appearance, it is more substantial than it appears at first glance. The inherent nature of S scrolls offers a bit of stretch (the ends are flexible because they aren't glued). Holding a curious child in your arms while wearing this pendant may not be the best idea, thinking of the way babies delight in reaching for shiny objects. If you prefer to skip the concern and make a very sturdy but slightly larger pendant, create the S scrolls from double-thickness strips. Keep in mind, however, that rolling a two-layer strip requires more finger pressure. Also, a thicker strip will most likely not fit into a slotted tool, so you will need to use a needle tool.

1 Roll 1 S scroll using a 2½" (6.5 cm) strip with the metallic edge facing up (**Figures 1 and 2**).

2 Roll 19 S scrolls using 2½" (6.5 cm) strips with the metallic edge facing down (**Figure 3**).

3 Make 4 domed tight coils using 2½" (6.5 cm) strips. Glue them together in a diamond shape (**Figure 4**).

4 Position the domed tight coils on a nonstick work board with the S scroll from step 1 with the metallic edge facing up (**Figure 5**). Arrange the remaining S scrolls, also with the metallic edge facing up, in a circular shape as shown to complete the pendant shape (**Figure 6**).

note: *You will most likely need to rearrange the scrolls slightly while gluing to maintain the circular formation.*

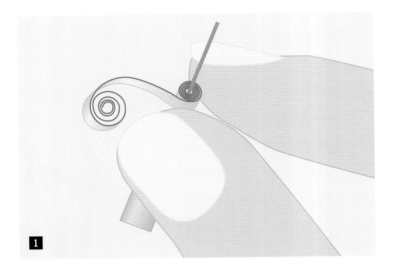

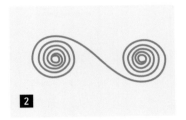

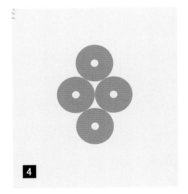

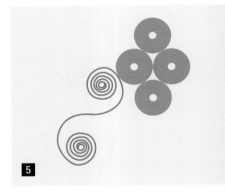

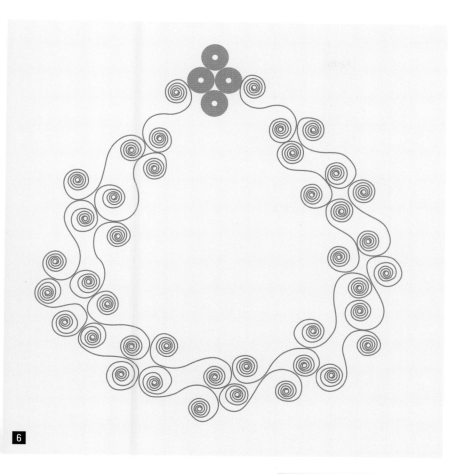

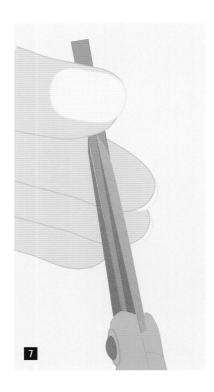

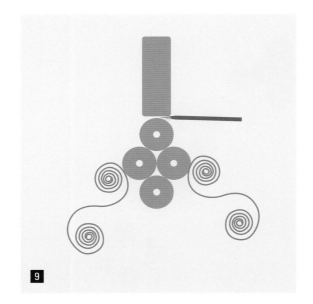

5 Make a metallic-paper bail: Trim the width of a ⅛" × 3" (3 mm × 7.5 cm) strip of pearlized gold quilling paper so that it is slightly narrower than ⅛" (3 mm) **(Figure 7)**. (This gives a finer look in proportion to the scale of the pendant.) Fold down one end of the strip about ¼" (6 mm) and wrap the strip around the initial fold 4 times **(Figure 8)**. Glue the end and trim the excess paper. Apply a tiny amount of glue to the strip end inside the coil to hold it in place. Glue this bail at the top of the domed tight coil cluster **(Figure 9)**.

6 When the glue is dry enough to safely handle the pendant, turn it over and apply a small dot of glue with the tip of a pin or paper-piercing tool on each join as reinforcement. Allow these dots to dry.

7 Apply a light coating of fixative with a watercolor brush to the back of the finished pendant, taking care to not overly saturate the scrolls as this would cause them to swell. Wait a few minutes and apply a second light coat. Allow the pendant to dry completely, preferably overnight.

8 Slide a necklace chain through the paper bail.

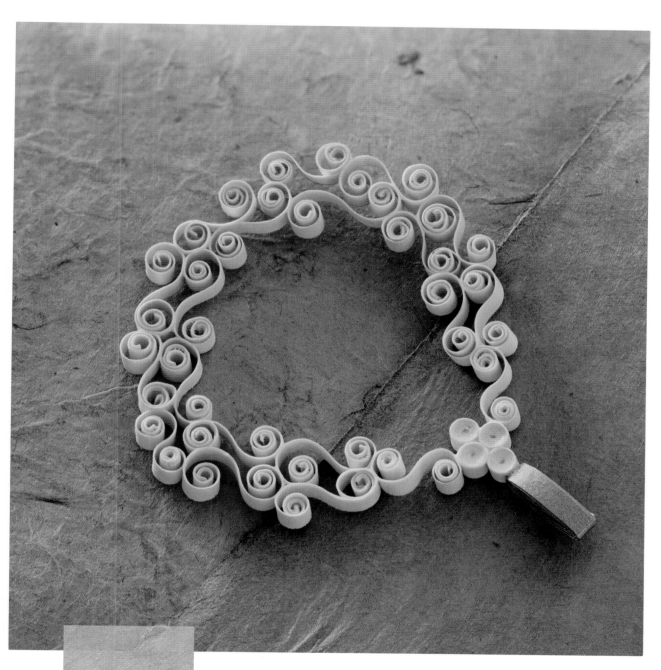

Attaching the bail to the diamond of domed tight coils ensures a secure connection when hanging from your chosen chain.

Enhanced Metal PENDANT

FINISHED SIZE
Pendant measures ¾"
× 1⅝" (2 cm × 4.1 cm).

SHAPES USED
Marquise

Teardrop

Domed tight coil

MATERIALS
Black with silver edge
quilling paper

Silver-tone pendant
blank

Silver-tone necklace
of choice

TOOLS
Quilling tool

Glue

Crafter's Pick The
Ultimate glue

Small scissors

Ruler

Fine-tip tweezers

Ball-head pins

Paper-piercing tool

⅛" (3 mm) dowel

Nonstick work board

Plastic lid or fine-tip
glue bottle

Damp cloth or
paper towel

Here, I've transformed a plain keychain that came with a handbag into a one-of-a-kind fashion statement by dressing up the smooth surface with a quilled design. The arrangement of coils is small enough to sit evenly on the slightly curved surface. If the quilling had been made just a little larger to cover the opening at the top, a pin back could have been glued onto the reverse side to wear the keychain as a brooch instead. A variety of metal pendant and pin blanks, as well as earring bezels, can be found at most craft supply stores. I like to adhere quilling securely to nonporous surfaces using Crafter's Pick The Ultimate. This glue creates a strong bond between paper and metal.

1

1 Roll a 2½" (6.5 cm) strip around a dowel that is a bit less than ⅛" (3 mm) in diameter. Slide this tiny ring coil off the dowel and pinch it to create a teardrop ring coil **(Figure 1)**. Glue the end and trim the excess paper. Then glue the loose end in place inside the teardrop ring coil.

2 Make two 1½" (3.2 cm) domed tight coils using ⅛" (3 mm) wide strips that have been trimmed slightly along the length **(Figure 2)**. Using the ⅛" (3 mm) strips, make eight 3" (7.5 cm) marquise coils, two 2½" (6.5 cm) teardrop coils, three 2" (5 cm) teardrop coils, and two 2" (5 cm) domed tight coils **(Figure 3)**.

3 On a nonstick work board, assemble the top portion of the design by gluing a set of three 3" (7.5 cm) marquise coils above and below the teardrop ring coil with a 1½" (3.2 cm) domed tight coil positioned on each side of the teardrop ring coil as shown **(Figure 4)**.

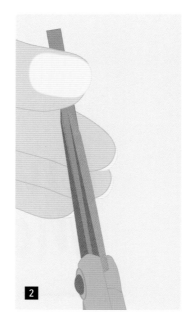

2

3

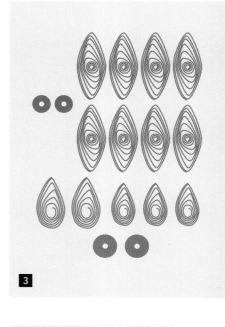

4

5

4 Glue the components together in the order listed to make up the lower half of the design:

a. Glue together two 3" (7.5 cm) marquise coils with a 2" (5 cm) teardrop positioned between them. Glue a 2" (5 cm) domed

6

7

8

tight coil at the top of the 2"
(5 cm) teardrop and another
2" (5 cm) domed tight coil at
the bottom of the 3" (7.5 cm)
marquise pair **(Figure 5)**.

b. Glue one 2½" (6.5 cm) teardrop
on each side of the bottom
domed tight coil with the points
facing outward **(Figure 6)**.

c. Glue one 2" (5 cm) teardrop
between each 2½" (6.5 cm)
teardrop and 3" (7.5 cm) marquise
with the points facing outward
(Figure 7). Let the glue dry
completely.

5 Pour a shallow layer of
Crafter's Pick The Ultimate
glue into a plastic lid. Use
tweezers to pick up the bottom
section of glued coils and touch
the underside to the glue. Then,

referring to **Figure 8**, place it on the
pendant surface. Repeat with the
upper section. Allow the glue to dry
completely, preferably overnight.

tip: *Decide where to position
the quilling ahead of time, then
position it exactly on the first try to
avoid sliding it around on the metal
surface, as this would create a shiny
snail trail of glue.*

6 Slip a necklace through the
jump ring.

FINISHED SIZE
Pendant measures 1½"
× 1⅝" (3.8 × 4.1 cm).

SHAPES USED
Marquise coil

Teardrop coil

Domed tight coil

Marquise ring coil

MATERIALS
Ivory with gold edge
quilling paper

Gold-tone 5 mm
jump ring

Gold-tone necklace
chain of choice

TOOLS
Quilling tool

Glue

Small scissors

Ruler

Fine-tip tweezers

Ball-head pins

Paper-piercing tool

⅜" (1 cm) dowel

Nonstick work board

Plastic lid or fine-tip
glue bottle

Damp cloth or
paper towel

2 pairs of flat-nose or
chain-nose jewelry pliers

Fixative (optional)

Watercolor brush
(optional)

Court Jester

PENDANT

The shape of this art deco design with its tiny domed tight coils at the ends of the marquises and teardrops takes me straight back to childhood. I had a deck of cards that included a pair of zany-looking court jesters or jokers, who wore funny hats enhanced with pointed tips. Each tip was decorated with a brightly colored pom-pom. I can't help but think of the many card games my sister and I played on our living room rug each time I look at this pendant.

1 Make eighteen 4" (10 cm) marquise coils, two 4" (10 cm) teardrop coils, and nine 1½" (3.8 cm) domed tight coils **(Figure 1)**.

2 Roll a 5" (12.5 cm) strip around a ⅜" (1 cm) dowel to make a ring coil. Slide the ring coil off the dowel and pinch it at opposite points to form a marquise ring coil. Glue the end and trim the excess paper. Then glue the loose end in place inside the marquise ring coil **(Figure 2)**.

3 On a nonstick work board, assemble the components in the order listed. Glue together 4 marquise coils in a diamond shape, then glue the marquise ring coil on the point to form the base **(Figure 3)**. Glue together the remaining coils and teardrop coils as shown **(Figure 4)**. Glue the domed tight coils on the tips of the marquise coils as shown **(Figure 5)**.

4 When the glue has dried enough for the pendant to be handled, turn it over and apply a dot of glue with the tip of a pin or paper-piercing tool on each join as reinforcement. Allow the glue to dry. Brush a light coating of fixative on the back of the pendant, if desired.

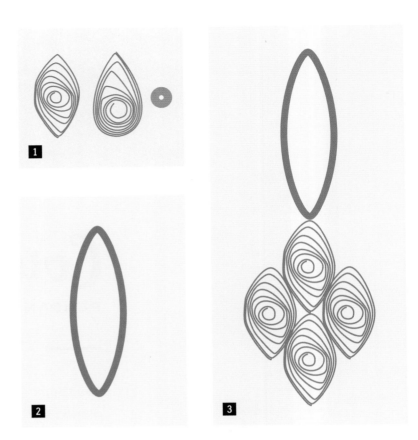

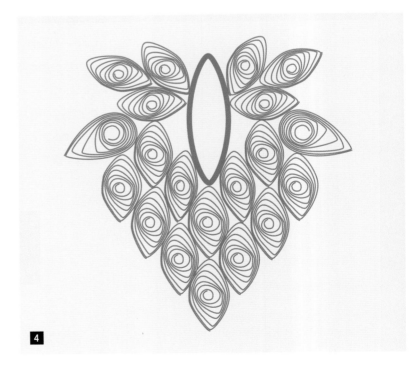

5

5 When the glue and fixative have dried completely, preferably overnight, use 2 pairs of jewelry pliers to twist open the jump ring and slide it through the marquise ring coil. Reverse the twisting motion to close it. Slide a necklace chain through the jump ring.

The tiny tight coils on the marquise tips are held securely in place with an extra dot of glue.

FINISHED SIZE
Each earring measures
1⅛" × 1⅜" (2.8 × 3.5 cm).

SHAPES USED
Teardrop coil

Marquise coil

Domed tight coil

MATERIALS
Black with silver edge
quilling paper

2 silver-tone 6 mm
jump rings

2 silver-tone 4 mm
jump rings

2 silver-tone ear wires

TOOLS
Quilling tool

Glue

Small scissors

Ruler

Fine-tip tweezers

Ball-head pins

Paper-piercing tool

¼" (6 mm) dowel

Nonstick work board

Plastic lid or fine-tip
glue bottle

Damp cloth or
paper towel

2 pairs of flat-nose or
chain-nose jewelry pliers

Fixative (optional)

Watercolor brush
(optional)

Art Deco

EARRINGS

While these earrings are a bit more ornate
than the Court Jester Pendant due to their
longer design, they can be worn with it as a
set if that's your fashion style.

FOR EACH EARRING:

1 Make four 4" (10 cm) teardrop coils, four 2½" (6.5 cm) teardrop coils, two 2" (5 cm) teardrop coils, four 4" (10 cm) marquise coils, and seven 1½" (3.8 cm) domed tight coils **(Figure 1)**.

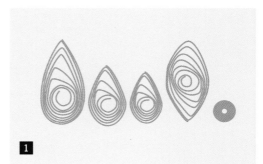

note:: The teardrop coils are placed as pairs with their inner coils rotating in opposite directions. To achieve this look, roll half of each teardrop coil pair with the metallic edge facing upward on the tool and the other half of the pair with the metallic edge facing downward.

2 Roll a 3¼" (8.5 cm) strip around a ¼" (6 mm) dowel. Slide this ring coil off the dowel and pinch it at opposite points to form a marquise ring coil **(Figure 2)**. Glue the end and trim the excess paper. Then glue the loose end in place inside the coil.

3 On a nonstick work board, assemble the components together as follows: Glue together the four 4" (10 cm) marquise coils as shown, then glue one end of the marquise ring coil to the point of the top marquise **(Figure 3)**. Glue the teardrop coils around the marquise ring coil as shown with the 4 large 4" (10 cm) teardrop coils positioned in pairs on each side and the 2 smaller 2" (5 cm) teardrop coils placed between them **(Figure 4)**. (Note the direction of the teardrop coils when placing them.) Glue the domed tight coils in place as shown **(Figure 5)**.

4 When the glue has dried enough for the earring to be handled, turn it over and apply a small dot of glue with the tip of a pin or paper-piercing tool on each join as reinforcement. Allow the glue to dry. Brush a light coating of fixative on the back of the earring, if desired. Allow the earrings to dry completely; preferably overnight.

5 Use 2 pairs of jewelry pliers to twist open a 6 mm jump ring and slip it through the marquise ring coil. Reverse the twisting motion to close the jump ring. Open a 4 mm ring and slip it onto the first jump ring. Slip an ear wire onto the open jump ring. Close the jump ring.

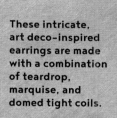

These intricate, art deco–inspired earrings are made with a combination of teardrop, marquise, and domed tight coils.

FINISHED SIZE
Pendant measures
1¾" × 2" (4.5 × 5 cm).

SHAPES USED
Shaped marquise

Domed tight coil

Ring coil

MATERIALS
Ivory with gold edge
quilling paper

Pearlized gold quilling
paper (for the bail)

Necklace chain of choice

TOOLS
Quilling tool

Glue

Small scissors

Ruler

Fine-tip tweezers

Ball-head pins

Paper-piercing tool

⅝" (1.5 cm) dowel

1" (2.5 cm) dowel

Nonstick work board

Plastic lid or fine-tip
glue bottle

Damp cloth or
paper towel

Fixative (optional)

Watercolor brush
(optional)

Double Ring PENDANT

This pendant often makes people stop
and do a double take. Because the design
is quite dense, the brilliant shine catches
their attention. And then when I tell them
it's made of paper, their eyes really light up.
"Paper? That's amazing!"

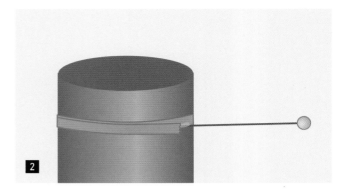

1 Using the ivory with gold edge quilling paper, make eighteen 4½" (11.5 cm) shaped marquise coils, twenty-nine 1½" (3.8 cm) domed tight coils, one 2" (5 cm) domed tight coil, and one 2¼" (5.7 cm) domed tight coil **(Figure 1)**.

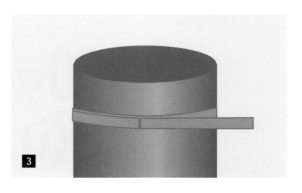

2 Make one ⅝" (1.5 cm) diameter ring coil by rolling a 15" (38 cm) strip with a torn end around a ⅝" (1.5 cm) dowel. Glue the torn end in place **(Figure 2)**. Slide the ring coil off the dowel and set aside.

3 Make one 1" (2.5 cm) diameter ring coil by rolling a 25" (63.5 cm) strip around a 1" (2.5 cm) dowel and gluing the torn end in place **(Figure 3)**.

note: *To make a 25" (63.5 cm) strip, you can either join strips by gluing torn ends together to make one long strip or butt and glue cut ends together while rolling.*

4 Glue the shaped marquise coils into 6 groups of 3 **(Figure 4)**. Glue the groups around the outer edge of the largest ring coil, spacing them evenly along the sides with a ⅜" (1 cm) gap at the top and bottom as shown **(Figure 5)**.

5 Glue a 1½" (3.8 cm) domed tight coil next to each of the marquise groupings as shown **(Figure 6)**.

6 Referring to **Figure 7**, glue together a column of 3 domed tight coils measuring 2¼" (5.7 cm), 2" (5 cm), and 1½" (3.8 cm) in descending size. Glue this column to the bottom center of the largest ring coil.

7 Glue the remaining twenty-two 1½" (3.8 cm) domed tight coils around the circumference of the ⅝" (1.5 cm) ring coil, leaving a small space for the paper bail **(Figure 8)**. Then glue this ring coil inside the top of the 1" (2.5 cm) ring coil.

8 When the glue has dried enough to handle the pendant, cut a 4½" (11.5 cm) strip of pearlized gold quilling paper that is slightly narrower than ⅛" (3 mm) **(Figure 9)**. Referring to **Figure 10**, make a paper bail by folding down ½" (1.3 cm) at one end of the strip and wrap the strip 3 times around itself and the 2 ring coils. Pinch the ring to create a teardrop ring coil **(Figure 11)**, then glue the end in place on the back of the coil, and trim the excess paper. Glue the loose end in place inside the teardrop ring coil.

9 Turn the pendant over and apply a small dot of glue with the tip of a pin or paper-piercing tool on each join as reinforcement.

10 When the glue has dried, brush the back side with a thin coating of fixative, if desired. Allow the pendant to dry completely, preferably overnight.

11 Slide a necklace chain through the paper bail.

9

10

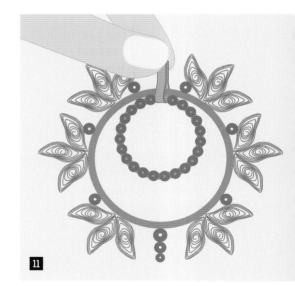

11

The depth of the Double Ring Pendant is created by a circle of domed tight coils glued on top of the inner ring coil.

FINISHED SIZE
Pendant is 1⅞" (4.8 cm)
in diameter.

SHAPES USED
Ring coil

Domed oval tight coil

Tight coil

Triangle ring coil

MATERIALS
Ivory with silver edge
quilling paper

Pearlized silver
quilling paper

Silver-tone 6 mm
jump ring

Silver-tone necklace
chain of choice

TOOLS
Quilling tool

Glue

Small scissors

Ruler

Fine-tip tweezers

Ball-head pins

Paper-piercing tool

1½" (3.8 cm) dowel

¼" (6 mm) dowel

Nonstick work board

Plastic lid or fine-tip
glue bottle

Damp cloth or
paper towel

2 pairs of flat-nose or
chain-nose jewelry pliers

Fixative (optional)

Watercolor brush
(optional)

Wallflower Wreath PENDANT

The solidity of this sweet masterpiece is a nice contrast to the delicate blossoms that are reminiscent of wallflowers. Yes, there really is a wallflower. But you certainly won't be one when you wear this shining pendant! The beautiful metallic-edge paper practically glows when it is coiled tightly. In addition, the flowers are made with varied strip widths that provide dimension. An underlying ring coil stabilizes the design. While it can be time-consuming to roll and assemble such small bits of paper, I don't think you'll regret the results of your labor. Tweezers are invaluable in picking up and positioning the coils. Also be sure to keep a damp cloth close at hand to avoid the frustration of sticky fingers.

1 Roll a full-length (17" [43.2 cm]) ivory with silver edge strip around a 1½" (3.8 cm) dowel. Glue the bluntly cut end. Butt and glue a second full-length ivory with silver edge strip against it and continue rolling. Glue the end. Butt and glue a 12" (30.5) strip of pearlized silver quilling paper against the previous end and wrap it around the ring coil twice (**Figure 1**). Cut the excess paper and glue the end. Slip the ring coil off the dowel. Put a dot of glue on the interior strip end to hold it in place.

2 Make the oval domed tight coil petals with ivory with silver edge strips. The wreath is composed of 3 sizes of 4-petal flowers—small, medium, and large. Make 6 flowers of each size. Note the length and width of the strips used:

■ The small flower petals are made with ⅛" × 2" (3 mm × 5 cm) strips that have been cut in half lengthwise (**Figure 2**). (Discard the nonmetallic edge halves.)

■ The medium flower petals are made with ⅛" × 3" (3 mm × 7.5 cm) strips that have been cut in half lengthwise. (Discard the nonmetallic edge halves.)

■ The large flower petals are made with ⅛" × 4" (3 mm × 10 cm) strips.

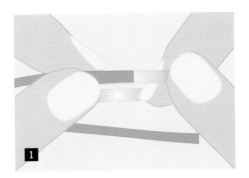

For each flower petal, roll a strip with a torn end on a slotted or needle tool to create a tight coil. Glue the torn end (**Figure 3**) and slide the coil off the tool. Indent the metallic side of the coil with a ball-head pin to create a domed tight coil with the shine on the cupped (interior) surface (**Figure 4**). With your fingers or tweezers, pinch the coil at opposite points to create an oval shape (**Figure 5**).

3 Assemble the oval domed tight coils into 4-petal flowers. Working with the dome (nonmetallic) side up, apply a tiny amount of glue to one end of an oval domed tight coil and adhere it to the end of another same-size oval domed tight coil as shown (**Figure 6**). Allow the glue to dry. Adhere the third and fourth oval domed tight coils to the first pair, one at a time (**Figure 7**) to complete the flower (**Figure 8**).

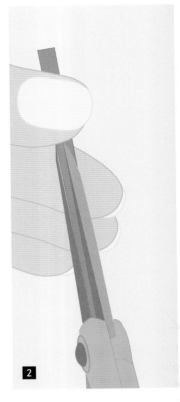

5

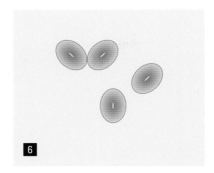

6

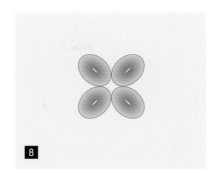

8

tip: Resist the impulse to glue all 4 coils together at once because they are sure to shift. Make 18 four-petal flowers total, 6 in each size.

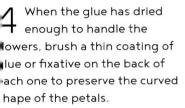

4 When the glue has dried enough to handle the flowers, brush a thin coating of glue or fixative on the back of each one to preserve the curved shape of the petals.

5 Create the flower centers. Cut the ⅛" (3 mm) ivory with silver edge strips in half lengthwise before rolling (refer to **Figure 2**). Discard the nonmetallic edge halves. Make six 1" (2.5 cm) tight coils for the small flowers, six 1¼" (3.2 cm) tight coils for the medium flowers, and six 1½" (3.8 cm) tight coils for the large flowers.

6 Pour a shallow layer of glue in a plastic lid. Using tweezers, dip the underside of each tight coil flower center in the glue, then place it on the appropriate size flower **(Figure 9)**.

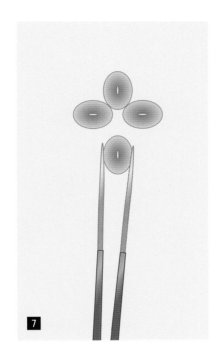

7

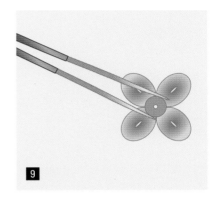

9

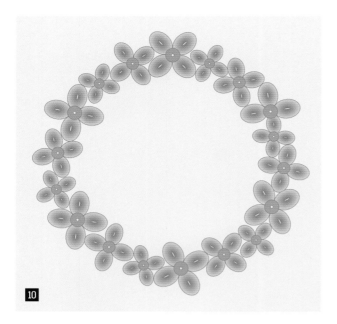

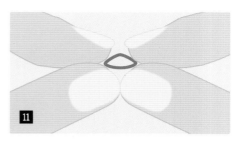

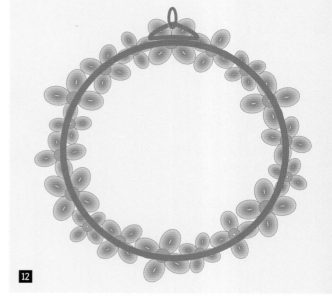

7 Glue the flowers side by side on the 1½" (3.8 cm) ring coil in an alternating small, medium, and large repeating pattern **(Figure 10)**. If they don't fit perfectly around the ring, create space by separating the flowers slightly or by removing a petal from one or two of the flowers. (One of my flowers has just 3 petals for this very reason. It's difficult to spot!)

8 Make a ring coil to use as a paper bail. Cut a 4½" (11.5 cm) strip of ivory with silver edge paper in half lengthwise. Discard the nonmetallic half and roll the silver edge half around a ¼" (6 mm) dowel. Slip this ring coil off the dowel, then pinch it at 3 points to create a triangle **(Figure 11)**. Glue the end and trim the excess paper. Apply a tiny amount of glue to the strip end inside the triangle to hold it in place.

9 Glue the triangle ring coil bail to the top of the underlying ring coil behind one of the largest flowers **(Figure 12)**.

10 Brush a light coating of fixative on the back of the pendant, if desired.

11 Use 2 pairs of jewelry pliers to twist open a jump ring and slide it through the bail. Reverse the twisting motion to close the jump ring. Slide a necklace chain through the jump ring.

The reverse side of the
Wallflower Wreath Pendant
shows the dimension of the
two-layer design.

Resources

U.S. SUPPLIERS

Custom Quilling
customquillingbydenise.com
*American and British
metallic-edge strips*

Quilling Supply Plus
quillingsupply.com
*American, British, and Dutch
metallic-edge strips*

Whimsiquills
whimsiquills.com
*American and British
metallic-edge strips*

Lake City Craft Co.
quilling.com
*American metallic-edge
strips (A Touch of Gold
and A Touch of Silver);
pearlized gold and
pearlized silver strips*

Little Circles
littlecirclesshop.net
*Bamboo dowels, stacked
ring-form kit*

Quilled Creations
quilledcreations.com
*Savvy Slotted Tool; Border
Buddy ring, square, and
triangle dowel tool*

Quilling Superstore
quillingsuperstore.com

U.K. SUPPLIERS

JJ Quilling Design
jjquilling.co.uk
British metallic-edge strips

Elderberry Crafts
elderberrycrafts.com
Dutch metallic-edge strips

JAPANESE SUPPLIER

Stripe
e-bison.ocnk.net
email: info@e-bison.co.jp
*Supplier of Superfine
Slotted tool*

Metric Conversion Chart

To Convert	To	Multiply By
Inches	Centimeters	2.54
Centimeters	Inches	0.4
Feet	Centimeters	30.5
Centimeters	Feet	0.03
Yards	Meters	0.9
Meters	Yards	1.1

Ann Martin has been quilling since 2002 when she was instantly captivated by a magazine article about the beautiful art of paper rolling. She learned the technique from books and via tips shared by helpful quillers she met online, and she gained valuable experience as a member of a design team for a quilling supply company. Ann was featured on the HGTV television show, *That's Clever,* and her tutorials have appeared in several books, including her own *All Things Paper and Creative Paper Quilling,* as well as craft, card-making, and handmade jewelry magazines. Ann's popular blog, *All Things Paper* (allthingspaper.net) features the work of remarkable paper artists and paper crafters around the world, in addition to her own designs. Her quilled jewelry has been exhibited in museums.

ACKNOWLEDGMENTS

I'd like to thank the team at F+W, Amelia Johanson, acquisitions editor, and Kerry Bogert, editorial director, for their sure guidance, and especially editor Jodi Butler for her quilling enthusiasm, attention to detail, and for always being at the other end of my emails. Heartfelt thanks to my husband, Bill, for his listening ear and can-do nature. Also, a special thank you to my online quilling friends, Licia Politis and Cecelia Louie. Although we have never met in person, I appreciate the many ways they have inspired me via our mutual love of paper.

Index

Elevate your jewelry-making skills with these must-have resources from Interweave

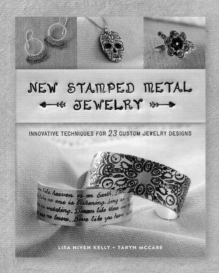

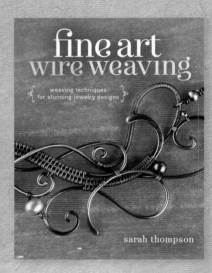

New Stamped Metal Jewelry

Innovative Techniques for 23 Custom Jewelry Designs

By Lisa Niven Kelly & Taryn McCabe

ISBN 978-1-63250-502-6

$24.99

Exploring Metal Jewelry

Wire Wrap, Rivet, Stamp & Forge Your Way to Beautiful Jewelry

By Tracy Stanley

ISBN 978-1-63250-456-2

$24.99

Fine Art Wire Weaving

Weaving Techniques for Stunning Jewelry Designs

By Sarah Thompson

ISBN 978-1-63250-025-0

$24.99

Available at your favorite retailer or interweave.com.

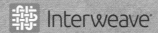 Interweave